Predictive Data Mining
A Practical Guide

Predictive Data Mining
A Practical Guide

Sholom M. Weiss

Rutgers University

Nitin Indurkhya

University of Sydney

Morgan Kaufmann Publishers, Inc.
San Francisco, California

Sponsoring Editor Michael B. Morgan
Production Manager Yonie Overton
Production Editor Cheri Palmer
Cover Design Ross Carron Design
Cover Photography Tommy Flynn/PHOTONICA
Composition Ed Sznyter, Babel Press
Technical Illustration Dartmouth Publishing, Inc.
Copyeditor Gary Morris
Proofreader Jennifer McClain
Printer Edwards Brothers, Inc.

Morgan Kaufmann Publishers, Inc.
Editorial and Sales Office
340 Pine Street, Sixth Floor
San Francisco, CA 94104-3205
USA
Telephone 415 / 392-2665
Facsimile 415 / 982-2665
E-mail mkp@mkp.com
Web site http://www.mkp.com
Order toll free 800 / 745-7323

02 01 00 99 98   5 4 3 2 1

Library of Congress Cataloging-in-Publication Data is available for this book.
ISBN 1-55860-403-0

Table of Contents

Preface

In an age of the Internet, intranets and data warehouses, the fundamental paradigms of classical data analysis are ripe for change. As storage and retrieval technology has advanced to the point where the main goals of relational databases—instant data recording and extremely rapid responses to queries—are well within reach, and as the amount of data stored in existing information systems has mushroomed, a new set of objectives for data management has emerged. Very large collections of data—millions or even hundreds of millions of individual records—are now being compiled into centralized data warehouses, allowing analysts to make use of powerful methods to examine data more comprehensively. In theory, "big data" can lead to much stronger conclusions for data-mining applications, but in practice many difficulties arise. This book reviews both classical and state-of-the-art techniques for extracting, transforming and organizing enormous quantities of raw data to facilitate a high-dimensional search for predictive solutions.

As we have listened to many others describe their concepts of data mining, it is clear that we are far from a universal agreement on the best methods for data mining or even what constitutes data mining. Is data mining a form of statistics or is it a revolutionary new concept? Do we start over, or can we benefit from the many years of multidisciplinary research on data analysis? In our view, most data-mining problems are an excellent fit to the classical problem of prediction from prior samples. A prediction problem simply means that data are collected over time and the correct answers (sometimes discovered much later) are stored with previous cases. The objective is to find patterns in the data that give accurate answers on new cases. Applications such as credit risk analysis, user profiling for marketing, or therapeutic outcomes analyses readily fit this model. To us, prediction is the heart of data mining, a field that is still emerging.

Besides emphasizing predictive data mining, this book also anticipates an active role for the human expert. We do not expect the machine to process big data without human guidance. The human has a critical role to play in formulating problems and preparing data. While we state what is scientifically known, we also conclude that a major artistic component remains. Best results are achieved by balancing both the knowledge of the human experts in describing problems and goals with the search capabilities of machines, sometimes running for lengthy periods of time on a single application.

Anyone owning, building, or thinking of building a data warehouse should find this book helpful in preparation for the technical and intellectual challenges associated with putting big data to work. A formal background in statistics or mathematics is not required. The material in this book is suitable for a graduate computer science course on data mining.

The chapters are organized as follows. In Chapter 1, the types of problems and goals suitable for predictive data mining are described. In Chapter 2, we discuss how to evaluate performance so that one is not misled by overly optimistic expectations. The human role, in organizing the data-mining effort and its goals and tasks, is presented in Chapter 3. Chapter 4 describes techniques for reducing the dimensions of massive quantities of data to manageable proportions. The prediction methods are reviewed in Chapter 5 and applied in Chapter 6. Instead of simulated data, proprietary data are used, and real-world case studies are presented in Chapter 7. How can the reader verify that these techniques are valid and can work successfully on their applications? Try our software option, which is available at http://www.data-miner.com or at http://www.mkp.com/books_catalog/1-55860-403-0.asp.

Special thanks are due to Rajesh Dube, who supported this work with a fascinating set of data-mining and networking applications.

1

What Is Data Mining?

Data mining is the search for valuable information in large volumes of data. It is a cooperative effort of humans and computers. Humans design databases, describe problems and set goals. Computers sift through data, looking for patterns that match these goals. Predictive data mining is a search for very strong patterns in big data that can generalize to accurate future decisions.

The classical model of data for prediction is a sample of cases. Potential measurements called *features* are specified, and these features are uniformly measured over many *cases*. For example, a prominent application of data mining is credit analysis for small business loans. Banks maintain databases of their loans, keeping both current and historical records. The criteria used to evaluate the risk of loans to small businesses are described in terms of features. These include features measuring a business's financial condition, such as recent profits and outstanding debt, or more personal features, such as the business owner's personal credit history. A case is a record of a specific loan to a small business. Hoping to reduce the risk of nonpayment, banks mine these data to find patterns of credit risk that are likely to hold for future loans. For each case, a goal or label is recorded, indicating the correct answer. The case label in the loan example is whether the loan was repaid, which is readily recorded as a zero or one. Alternatively, the case label could be the actual profit and loss for each loan, and the objective is to minimize losses.

The technical mission of predictive data mining is to "learn" decision criteria for assigning labels to new unlabeled cases. For the loan

Cases	Business current in supplier payments?	...	Late or default on owner's personal loans?	Length of time in business	Goal: Loan repay or default
Yes	...	No	12 Years	Repay
Yes	...	Yes	6 Years	Default
...	...	...	...	...
No	...	No	3 Years	Repay

Figure 1.1: A Spreadsheet Example for Business Loan Data

example, the patterns should distinguish between the cases of repaid loans and those in default. Spreadsheet models of data, such as the loan example in Figure 1.1, are sufficient to describe data for prediction. These simple characterizations, augmented by automated "prediction methods," programs that find patterns in data, provide a rich world of problems and goals for predictive data mining.

1.1 Big Data

A defining characteristic of data mining is "big data." We have grown accustomed to rapidly increasing computer processing power and stable costs. The widespread availability of relatively inexpensive but powerful computing has led to another revolution, the storage of massive amounts of data in electronic form.

The spreadsheet model of data has two primary dimensions: the number of cases and the number of features. A secondary dimension is the number of distinct values. A complete probabilistic description requires knowledge of the joint probabilities of the features. In the study of small business loans, over 400 features are measured for each loan. What is the joint probability of a default given a high balance in the business's checking account, up-to-date payments to suppliers but a personal credit card limit exceeded by the owner and ...?

Even with big data, sufficient cases are never available to determine these probabilities exactly. For most applications, many features are unimportant. Out of 400 features measured for a sample of 5,000 small business loans, about 10 were effective predictors. Surprisingly, the personal credit history of the business owner is more predictive than the financial records of the business. Can a spreadsheet be prepared with fewer features than the available number of features? Without detailed knowledge of the application, how can this be determined? It is easy to demonstrate the difficulties of high dimensions and big data even with enormous computing resources.

We address these dimensionality issues in this book. Can we effectively mine big data? Which techniques safely reduce dimensions? Big data simplify the evaluation of results, but create many new problems for high-dimensional data mining.

1.1.1   The Data Warehouse

The big data revolution has begun. More and more organizations are moving data for decision support to a centralized resource known as a *data warehouse*. A storage model for data mining is illustrated in Figure 1.2. In a large organization, databases may be dispersed among subsidiary units, each recording potentially massive numbers of transactions. Knowledgeable specialists carefully design data warehouses, where data are extracted from these operational databases and centrally recorded. The data warehouse is not updated in real time, only at some frequency that balances operational efficiency and the need for timely data. The key idea is to make available to management the critical information that can be used for further analytical processing and decision making.

Raw data stored in databases are not necessarily in the best form for data mining. It's a big leap from transactional databases to configuring a centralized resource, the data warehouse, where data supportive to decision making are stored. A number of tasks, illustrated in Figure 1.3, are usually performed to move data from dispersed sources to a centralized warehouse.

- Extraction: Data are extracted from different sources in different formats.

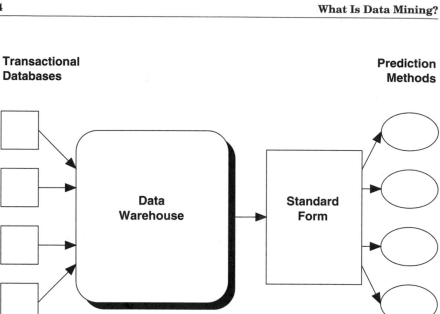

Figure 1.2: The Data Warehouse Model for Data Mining

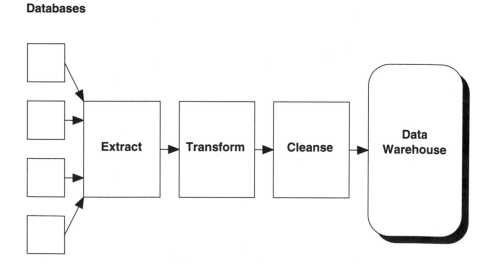

Figure 1.3: Moving Operational Data to the Warehouse

- Transformation: Data are transformed from raw data into data most suited for decision support. For example, each sale may be recorded, but a summary of sales per day may be the transformation best suited for decision support and a data warehouse.

- Cleansing: Erroneous records are eliminated and data fields are checked for consistency and missing values. Attempts are made to clean up the data by fixing errors or by discarding records.

- Integration: Data from multiple databases and other sources are integrated into the central warehouse.

Having a data warehouse does not necessarily resolve all data preparation issues. Data extracted from warehouses may need additional transformations to produce a uniform and standard presentation compatible with predictive data mining.

Very substantial research efforts have been expended in the development of improved prediction methods that search for patterns in the data. While there is a huge body of research literature on prediction methods and statistics, far less is known about data preparation issues. To a large extent, the organizational efforts for predictive data mining can be performed independently of prediction methods. These preparatory tasks are often more critical and time-consuming than applying prediction methods. For the small business loan example, the most elementary linear "credit scoring" model is used, where points are added for positive predictors of repayment and deducted for features suggesting increased risk of default. Reducing the need for extensive financial review and in-person interviews, a computed score above a threshold gains approval of the loan. In contrast to the simple application of the prediction method, extensive preparation and study of potential features are necessary to mine the data and reach an effective solution.

The growing utilization of data warehouses is an emerging phenomenon, and experience with mining them is limited. While alternative prediction methods are reviewed in Chapter 5, the main concerns are the preparation of data and the development of an overall problem-solving strategy. How can data extracted from a data warehouse be organized and transformed for effective data mining? Can massive amounts of data be reduced to their most predictive features and essential measures? Can a global data-mining strategy be specified that helps find the best answers?

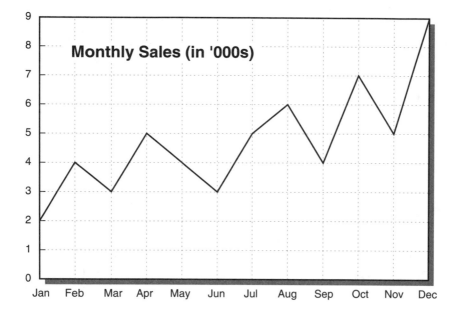

Figure 1.4: A Data Timeline

1.1.2   Timelines

A data warehouse can supply very large volumes of data, possibly millions of cases with hundreds of features. For many applications, the data
are not stationary and vary greatly over time. Possibilities range from
classical statistical sampling problems with stable populations, such
as those for many diagnostic problems, to *time-series* problems with
evolving trends and populations. For example, the monthly sales of a
hypothetical product are recorded in Figure 1.4. Many marketing and
business forecasting problems are time-series analyses with data sampled at fixed intervals of time. Overall, we can expect to find data-mining
problems that range over both extremes of stationary and nonstationary
data.

Database systems can store data with a time stamp, but general
data-mining programs expect to receive these data in some standard

form. From the perspective of database systems, the efficient storage and query of time-stamped information is a complex task. From a predictive data-mining perspective, the time-stamped data greatly increase the dimensions of problem solving in a completely different direction. Instead of cases with one measured value for each feature, cases have the same feature measured at different times.

Predictive data-mining methods prefer the classical sample and case model of data but have difficulties reasoning with time and its greatly increased dimensions. How can the data be transformed into lesser dimensions without losing information? Our approach to time analysis keeps the case model while increasing the flexibility to handle a much broader and more realistic group of problems. Raw, time-dependent data may need further transformations for predictive data mining. Such transformations can include specifying counts or ratios, or moving averages to summarize past events in a reduced feature space.

1.2   Types of Data-Mining Problems

Although data mining is an emerging field, it draws many of its basic principles from mature concepts in databases, machine learning and statistics. Table 1.1 is a list of some generic types of data-mining problems. We have divided these into two general categories: (a) *prediction* and (b) *knowledge discovery*. Prediction is arguably the strongest goal of data mining, has the greatest potential payoff and has the most precise description. Knowledge discovery is an all-encompassing label for many topics related to decision support. Prediction problems are described in terms of specific goals, which are related to past records with known answers. These are used to project to new cases. Knowledge discovery problems usually describe a stage prior to prediction, where information is insufficient for prediction. Knowledge discovery is complementary to predictive data mining, but is closer to decision support than decision making.

Applications like fraud detection, marketing, healthcare outcomes and investment analysis have been cited as fertile ground for data mining. What kinds of problems are these? They are all prediction problems. In the absence of superior knowledge about an application, these problems are solved by looking at past experience with known answers, and

Prediction	Knowledge Discovery
Classification	Deviation Detection
Regression	Database Segmentation
Time series	Clustering
	Association Rules
	Summarization
	Visualization
	Text mining

Table 1.1: Types of Data-Mining Problems

then projecting to new cases. Fraud is detected by looking for similar patterns in past examples of fraud. Marketing is directed to those potential customers who match the pattern of previous successful sales. Treatments are deemed cost-effective when they fit a pattern of success in previous patients. Investment decisions are made based on a pattern of prior gain.

When an application is not mature or does not have the potential for a predictive solution, knowledge discovery may be the goal. Many of these same knowledge discovery problems can be described in terms of a predictive model. Our book is about prediction, but the technical methods for solving these problems often overlap with those for knowledge discovery. Let's look in greater detail at the problem types of Table 1.1 to clarify the relationship of prediction to knowledge discovery.

- Prediction: The two central types of prediction problems are *classification* and *regression*. Samples of past experience with known answers (labels) are examined and generalized to future cases. The spreadsheet form described for the loan example is the conceptual data model for prediction problems. For classification, the answer is true or false; for example, the loan was repaid. For regression, the answer is a number; for example, the profit or loss on the loan. *Time series* is a specialized type of regression or occasionally classification problem, where measurements are taken over time for the same features; for example, the loan payments for each month are recorded and examined. Prediction from cases with known answers is the main focus of this book.

- Deviation Detection: Detecting changes from the norm has many analogs in statistical analysis. The classical technique for detecting differences is *significance testing*, where summary statistics like means and standard deviations are used to measure differences. These topics are reviewed in Chapter 2, and distance measures for computing the difference from multiple features and means are described in Section 4.2.2. As will be discussed in Chapter 2, significant differences, which are deviations from the norm, are not always strong enough for accurate prediction. A younger person may be a greater risk for loan default, but age may not be a strong predictor of default. Data mining may still be a valuable process for discovering increased probabilities or risks associated with various goals. From a prediction perspective, deviation detection is often related to low-prevalence events; for example, the number of defaults is small relative to the number of loans. Does it mean that predictive methods will fail on these problems? Not at all. Some deviation detection problems can be directly solved. In other instances, prediction methods can be adapted to situations where the cost of error is increased in one direction; for example, the cost of error for not predicting a default is greater than for not predicting repayment. With big data, one approach to managing different costs of errors is to assemble a sample where the key predictive goal is represented by a greater proportion of cases than actually occur, for example, equal numbers of default and repayment cases. Deviation detection is readily formulated as a prediction problem when samples of prior deviations can be collected.

- Database Segmentation: Sometimes, a larger problem is divided into smaller subproblems that form natural groupings. The larger database is decomposed into distinct groups. In the most common situation, the database may be segmented by a single feature. For example, a loan database or a marketing database could be segmented by age into mutually exclusive groups with the expectation that a distinct solution will be found for each group. How are the groups divided? Section 4.5 describes several procedures, based either on the known goals and answers stored for a case, like repayment or default, or on clusters of similar cases in the absence of answers.

- Clustering: Predictive data mining requires samples with known answers. What happens when these answers are unavailable? A data warehouse is loaded with data but no clear goals have been established. Careful formulation of goals in consultation with domain experts is crucial for predictive data mining. Yet, it is technically feasible to let computer programs roam the data, automatically grouping cases into clusters of similar cases. Automated procedures for clustering are a type of *exploratory analysis*, and results can be interesting but usually highly tentative and weaker than results for mining samples with known answers. Unlike database segmentation using a single variable, many features for the cases can be used to measure similarity. While clustering is a subject matter that can be investigated independent of prediction, one of the simplest and most effective clustering techniques is described in Section 4.5.1.2.

- Association Rules and Link Analysis: The natural language of databases is a form of logic where the terms are true or false. For example, find the patterns where loans are repaid, and present the answer in a logic format such as "Loans are repaid with 90% confidence when the proprietor has a personal history of timely credit card payments." These are associations in the form of decision rules. One major alternative model is a mathematical function. Logic methods for prediction, which use a form of association for describing solutions and patterns, including sequential links over time, are described in Section 5.4.2.

- Summarization and Visualization: A major goal of data mining is often described as "finding compact descriptions of data." By definition, most predictive data-mining methods, like the logic methods or mathematical function methods, find solutions that are much simpler than the full store of data in the warehouse. Otherwise, no generalizable patterns would emerge. While proposed predictive solutions usually have summarizing characteristics, these solutions are not always easily understood. One of the principal approaches to describing information is visualization. When data are not yet organized in some standard form with features and goals, visualization techniques are of primary interest for discovering new knowledge. When data are ready for prediction, visualization is often an explanatory adjunct, restricted by the high-dimensional spaces explored by predictive methods. The role of visualization relative to predictive methods is discussed in Chapter 5 with pointers to some innovative techniques in Section 6.9.

- Text Mining: The data warehouse may contain many types of information. Much of the contents may be text, ranging from text fields in records to complete documents. Predictive data-mining methods generally expect numbers for their data. Text data can be transformed into a form that is amenable to further processing by text-mining methods, and examples of these transformations are described in Section 3.6.

Some database systems and their mining software have overlapping functions that cross the boundaries of prediction and knowledge discovery. This is not surprising, because knowledge is a prerequisite for predictive data mining. From our perspective, though, prediction is a primary theme of data mining and can be used as a navigator for pursuing a very broad spectrum of related practical problems.

1.3　The Pedigree of Data Mining

Data mining draws on the concepts and methods of databases, statistics and machine learning. While big data is a common theme, each of these three areas has a somewhat different emphasis in its approach to data mining.

1.3.1　Databases

It is incontrovertible that databases are critical to everyday commerce, and computers routinely process and record massive numbers of transactions. Thus, data mining would seem to have a natural home in the database community.

Database researchers and vendors have the most successful track record in managing big data. Database software is real, not conjecture. Its commercial use is pervasive. The fundamental paradigm of database systems is the query model: You ask a question, and the system gives an answer. Data mining is just another form of query: "Which loans will default next year?" A critical expectation for database systems is efficiency. Responses to queries must be quick, typically measured in seconds. Rapid response implies efficient retrieval of information. Careful attention is given to the database organization with appropriate links to different categories of information. To a database specialist, a database is much more than a big file.

However, these very strengths of processing big data create obstacles for data mining. Considering only efficient responses may eliminate many approaches that can provide valuable results, results that are not needed in real time. The database vendor maintains much control over the consumer. In response to new demands, a database specialist might say, "That's an interesting possibility, but it is not yet available." For example, temporal databases are only now emerging from the traditional relational model employed by most current database systems. The database vendor will argue for patience; they will eventually add a new program routine. Critics may argue that not all questions can be naturally represented as a query. The big-file view of the spreadsheet model may be simplistic and inefficient, but it is amenable to the specialized data transformations that are often necessary in data mining. The advent of data warehouses, where key information from many sources is pooled, has greatly increased the potential for data mining.

1.3.2 Statistics

Why shouldn't the statistician be in charge of data mining? Who knows more about the rigorous and scientific examination of data? Over many years, statisticians have developed the methods that are used daily to evaluate hypotheses and to determine whether differences can be ascribed to random chance. At the heart of statistics are models of data and methods of prediction that are supported by formal statistical theory.

These enormous strengths may also be weaknesses. Classical statistical models, dominated by linear models, are now seen as models for modest, not big, data. Setting rigorous standards for modeling and statistical proof, sqtatistical methods may have restricted the horizons of data mining to easily computable approaches. In a computer age, statistical models can be too efficient, often coming at the expense of too many simplifying assumptions.

Some statistical models are competitive with those developed by computer scientists and may overlap in concept. Still, classical statistics may be saddled with a timidity that is not up to the speed of modern computers.

1.3.3 Machine Learning

In this category, we lump the many prediction methods developed by computer scientists outside of the statistics community. Here the basic approach is to specify some interesting model like a decision tree or neural net, and then enumerate and search through the possibilities. Perhaps some simplifications are necessary, but the search or optimization perspective is quite natural for computer scientists. Oblivious to statistical tradition, computer scientists have explored numerous new approaches, many of which are well suited to big data and more powerful computing. These innovative prediction methods often produce strong empirical results.

It is reasonable to expect substantial cooperation among the different research communities. Data-mining conferences draw researchers and practitioners from each of these diverse fields. Data warehouses are the home of big data, but many prediction methods expect a specialized *standard form* that usually differs from the stored database representation. Databases are well organized, efficient and proven, but this organization is not necessarily the best for predictive data mining. Thus, divergent views of mining may continue until a more common perspective is reached.

Which view is correct? There is no need to take a position, and there may be no single correct answer. Instead, we can examine the issues that are critical to getting the best results.

1.4 Is Big Better?

Despite its high dimensions, big data should be considered highly advantageous. If the numbers of cases are overwhelming, subsets of cases can readily be substituted during data mining. In the classical environment of data analysis where data are in short supply, a dilemma arises. While the available cases are needed to "train" the prediction method, additional test cases are also necessary for evaluating predictive performance. With only one modest sample available, a classical problem of prediction is to maximize effective use of data in short supply for both training and testing. With big data, this problem is removed from center stage.

1.4.1 Strong Statistical Evaluation

Big data leave plenty of cases for evaluation. Prior to the application of the prediction methods, a large number of cases are reserved for testing, and the test data are not examined by the machine during the training process. For big data, the desirability of complicated simulations of test data is diminished, as are worries about the affordability of devoting large portions of the original data to testing. A small percentage of the data may still consist of thousands of cases, which is adequate for most testing scenarios.

Formal statistical significance tests are also far more accurate because confidence in their results is directly proportional to the number of test cases. Intuitively, we know that results are much more palatable, and far less likely to be due to chance when they have been thoroughly tested on cases not seen during training.

1.4.2 More Intensive Search

In theory, most prediction methods should be happy with big data. They have the potential to extract more information from data during training. If data mining is a search through a space of possibilities, then big data suggest many more possibilities to enumerate and evaluate. If predictive data mining is a process of estimation, then many more samples are available for estimates of future performance. Big data are particularly important for low-prevalence applications.

The potential for increased enumeration and search is counterbalanced by practical limitations. Putting aside the dimensional and computational issues, a more exhaustive search may also increase the risk of finding a single low-probability solution that evaluates well, but may not meet future expectations.

The search paradigm for predictive data mining is not the same as other forms of computer-based search, for example, those used in the game of chess. The computer search is not for a single triumphal move. Instead, many conflicting choices are balanced in their support of a likely pattern of behavior. This type of search, with combined support from multiple cases, makes it much more likely that effective solutions can be found in both large and reduced search spaces.

1.4.3 More Controlled Experiments

Prediction methods that search a space of candidate solutions have many choices to make. Multiple solutions of varying complexity can be enumerated. Without experimentally comparing the alternatives on data from a specific application, the best predictive performance may not be achieved. While prediction methods have default settings that often work well, there are many potential improvements. Data miners become "tuners" who are willing to explore the alternatives relative to a specific collection of data.

With big data, the tuning approach is particularly reasonable. Data are sufficient for evaluation and comparison even when the parameters are tuned for the same basic method. The larger the set of test cases, the less worry about reusing the same test data many times. With big data, a subset of cases can be set aside for tuning or test purposes to determine what is best for a specific application.

1.4.4 Is Big Necessary?

While big data have the potential for better results, there is no guarantee that they are more predictive than small data. For example, if a dataset is composed of a computer-generated set of random numbers, no matter how big the data, nothing of value will be found. From a data perspective, the data are big. From a knowledge perspective, they are small and useless. Given high-dimensional data, a central question is whether it can be determined, prior to searching for all solutions in all dimensions, that a method has exhausted its potential for prediction. The worst case may be data with no predictive value. More commonly encountered is a solution induced from a subset of available features or cases that continues to be the most predictive even when the search space is enlarged to include more features or cases.

1.5   The Tasks of Predictive Data Mining

Predictive data mining is goal directed. Representative samples of cases with known answers, summarizing past experiences in meeting these goals, must be in place for predictive mining. Each application has a motivating story that should lead naturally to a problem specification. Given a story and a data warehouse, predictive data mining can be decomposed into four major tasks:

- Phase 1: Data Preparation

- Phase 2: Data Reduction

- Phase 3: Data Modeling and Prediction

- Phase 4: Case and Solution Analyses

In general, these tasks are performed in this order, and once a phase is completed, it is often not repeated. These are general guidelines for predictive data mining in an orderly fashion. There is no penalty for diverging from these ordered steps or repeating previous steps. Let's review these four phases.

1.5.1   Data Preparation

A most critical step in data mining is the preparation and transformation of data. This task, to be described in detail in Chapter 3, often receives little attention in the research literature, mostly because it is considered too application specific. An alternative view, taken in this book, is that data preparation largely can be described independently of an application and a prediction method. The remaining phases of data

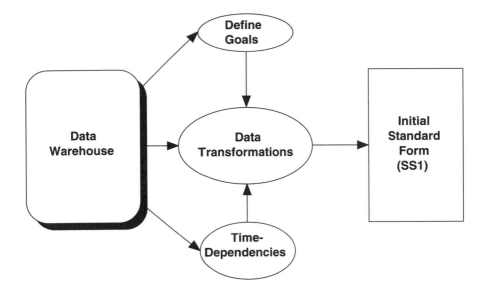

Figure 1.5: Data Preparation

mining, such as data reduction, readily flow from a general model of prepared data.

Figure 1.5 describes the principal relationships for data preparation, where the raw data are transformed into SS1, the first complete spreadsheet. We have adopted a *standard spreadsheet form* for a model of data, and this constrains the original data to a relatively simple uniform representation that is almost universally acceptable to techniques of predictive data mining. Some of the data preparation tasks can be performed during the design of the data warehouse, but many specialized transformations may be needed when a predictive analysis is requested.

Raw data are not always best for predictive data mining. Many transformations may be needed to produce features with useful predictive value. Counting in different ways, using different sampling sizes, taking important ratios, varying window sizes and moving averages all can contribute to better results. Do not expect that the machine will find the best set of transformations without human assistance. Some of these

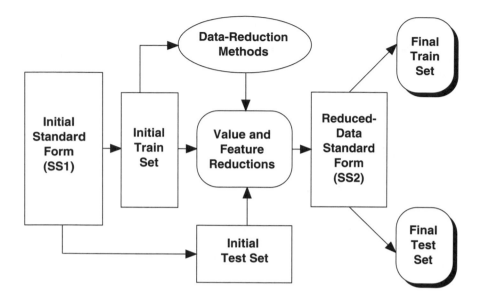

Figure 1.6: Data Reduction

transformations may be designed into the data warehouse. Many others may not be anticipated until mining actually proceeds.

1.5.2   Data Reduction

The theoretical advantages of big data for training and testing are obvious, but in practice, the data may be too big. The dimensions can exceed the capacity of a prediction program, or it may take too long to process and produce a solution. This is especially true when a solution is reached by an iterative process where repeated experiments are performed. Once the data are in a standard form, there are a number of effective techniques to reduce dimensions. These are discussed in detail in Chapter 4.

Figure 1.6 illustrates the principal steps for data reduction. Given the standard-form spreadsheet, SS1, the data are reduced by either features or values, and a new spreadsheet, SS2, is produced. When the dimensions of the standard form are within acceptable bounds, data reduction may be bypassed. The data-reduction techniques of Chapter 4 are the available tools for high-dimensional feature spaces. The experiments of Chapter 6 demonstrate that such methods can be useful and effective in reducing dimensions.

Once the data have been reduced to a new spreadsheet, SS2, the data can officially be divided into train and test cases. Test cases are critical to evaluation of results, which is the subject of Chapter 2. The next two phases of predictive data mining are iterative tasks. Choices and interpretations cannot be made without accurate estimates of predictive performance.

1.5.3 Data Modeling and Prediction

Many automated methods are available for predictive data mining. A representative collection of the strongest ones, and their models of data, are described in Chapter 5. Independent of specific prediction methods, successful data mining may require many experiments to tune the method for best predictive performance or other desirable solution characteristics.

A search space could be defined consisting of combinations of parameters and option settings. These combinations could be tried in sequence and the variation that leads to the best results is selected. However, this approach to finding solutions is unrealistic. Moreover, experience suggests that relatively few parameters have a major impact on results. The typical approach to iterative tuning on big data is indicated in Figure 1.7. Many decisions can usually be made on a moderate and random subset of available cases without a full commitment to the solutions found on the subset of data.

1.5.4 Case and Solution Analyses

Having completed the preparatory work, we are ready to find solutions, such as those described in Chapters 6 and 7. With big data, and cases numbering in the tens of thousands, an exploratory, incremental or even adaptive approach is often preferred. The capacity of the prediction method must be considered as well as the potential time that might be consumed in finding a solution. Figure 1.8 illustrates an incremental approach to the analyses of solutions found for big data. Data mining with incremental and random samples of data is an effective strategy for

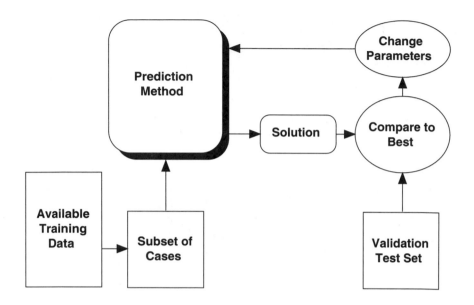

Figure 1.7: Iterative Data Modeling and Prediction

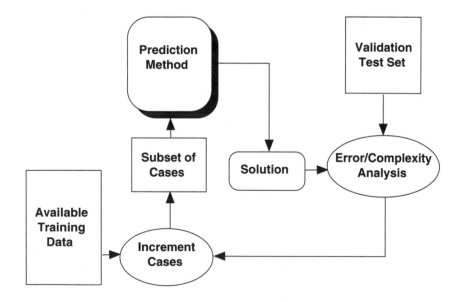

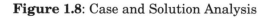

Figure 1.8: Case and Solution Analysis

coping with massive sets of data and is described in detail in Chapters 4, 5 and 6.

1.6   Data Mining: Art or Science?

The contributions of humans to data mining are often neglected. Results are dependent on the predictive value of the features. It is the human who specifies the set of features, who usually knows to discard the junk and who investigates how to transform the original features into better features. Volumes of papers are published on the scientific components of prediction methods and data mining. These are important papers that give results usually under controlled laboratory conditions with various theoretical assumptions. Topics where art predominates over science, like preparing the data or selecting and transforming the features, are rarely discussed. Comparative studies may find that many different prediction methods are competitive. The greatest gains in performance are often made by describing more predictive features.

The human has a critical design role to play in data mining. The success of the effort is dependent on the problem design. Once some results are found, the human must react to these results. Mining experiments may be tried with many variations. The data may be transformed in many different ways. Every possible variation cannot be tried, but those that are tried can be effectively evaluated. No universal best approach is describable for data mining; making good decisions is part art, part science. Our task in this book is to blend the art and science: to use the science when it is known and effective, and to offer guidance on many practical issues that are not readily quantified.

1.7   An Overview of the Book

In the remainder of the book, we consider these tasks of predictive data mining. Our analysis is almost exclusively from the data's perspective. What can be done to prepare the data and in what form? Are all the data needed or can dimensions be reduced by smoothing or eliminating some of the data? In Chapter 5, we discuss the prediction methods from a high-dimensional perspective. Alternative representations are reviewed, not mathematical derivations. Later, these concepts see action

on real data in a comparative study of alternative approaches to data
mining. We then leave the controlled setting used for scientific comparison and review our experiences on these same applications where many
design choices are made based on experience, not just comparison.

Here is an overview of the upcoming chapters:

- Chapter 2 reviews the statistics of evaluation and prediction for
  big data.

- Chapter 3 describes a standard form for data organization. It ex-
  amines several forms of raw data and considers transformations
  that may help improve results. Among the topics covered are data
  with strong time-dependencies and data described as free text.

- Chapter 4 reviews techniques for reducing data dimensions. Do we
  really need all these cases and features?

- Chapter 5 gives an overview of applied prediction methods that
  fall into three groups: (a) math, (b) distance and (c) logic methods.

- Chapter 6 presents a comparative study of the data-reduction tech-
  niques from Chapter 4 and the prediction methods of Chapter 5.
  The data studied are big data from the real-world problems of
  Chapter 7.

- Chapter 7 focuses on some proprietary real-world data mining efforts. It describes an organizational model for unifying the tasks
  of the previous chapters, and presents protocols for preparing data
  and organizing the mining effort. The organizational model is applied to the data-mining applications.

1.8   Bibliographic and Historical Remarks

Data mining and data warehouses are terms popularized by the database community and are now widely used computer jargon. The examples from the credit application are based on a vivid description of the
influence of computer credit scoring on banks' loan practices [Hansell,
1995].

Research on data mining has had a small but growing presence in
the database literature. The database perspective on mining is given

in [Agrawal, Imielinski and Swami, 1993]. Complexities of temporal databases are examined in [Tansel et al., 1993] and [Saraee and Theodoulidis, 1995]. The relational model has been the fundamental representation of data in commercial database systems. The divergence of requirements for retrieval versus mining has led to newer, multidimensional database models or enhanced relational models that can support time analysis and OLAP, online analytical processing [Baum, 1996].

The influence of networking on data mining, through the global Internet and local intranets, cannot be underestimated. Networks expand the possibilities for data capture, and data warehouses are a natural evolution to organize massive quantities of data [Kimball, 1996]. Once the data are in place, data mining follows. Vendor web pages on the Internet are a source of current information on these topics. A web search on key words such as data warehousing or mining will yield useful links. Examples of informative presentations can be found by following the links at www.data-miner.com.

The idea that data are more than input to statistical models, and can be manipulated to select a best solution, has its early roots in [Tukey, 1977]. Distinct research communities are working on prediction methods such as those described in Chapter 5. Our presentation emphasizes the technical concepts of predictive data mining with big data. General reviews of key issues for knowledge discovery in databases, including goals other than prediction, are found in [Fayyad, Piatetsky-Shapiro and Smyth, 1996; Brachman and Anand, 1996; Piatetsky-Shapiro, Brachman, Khabaza, Kloesgen and Simoudis, 1996].

2

Statistical Evaluation
for Big Data

Although the floodgates have opened to the onrushing tides of new data-mining methods, the role of classical statistics in the evaluation of results is undiminished. The quality of conclusions must be evaluated, and choices must be made among the many alternative ways of mining data. For big data, evaluation is much simpler, and in theory, conclusions are much stronger.

Our daily encounters with formal statistics are usually limited to reading about health-related risks or the results of polls. For data mining, expectations are that business applications predominate. For these commercial applications, the goal is financial gain, not publication in scientific journals demonstrating a significant difference between two test groups.

The jump from basic research to commercial application should not lead us to ignore the basic principles of evaluation. Rather, we consider how evaluation is done under idealized conditions, understand what motivates these approaches, and then consider whether these principles are useful for data mining. Even without any formal application of statistical models for evaluation, the underlying principles of evaluation are invoked whenever test data are used. Because big data move evaluations of results closer to idealized models, it's worth our time to examine a few concepts that are fundamental to sampling theory and its application.

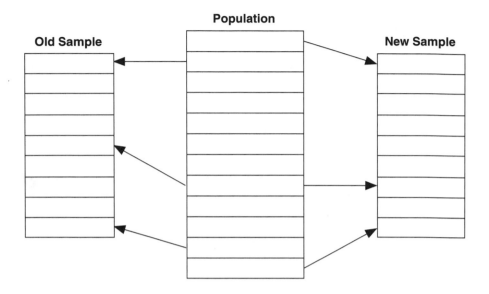

Figure 2.1: Random Sampling with Replacement

2.1 The Idealized Model

The spreadsheet data format used in previous examples describes big data in terms of rows of cases and columns of measurements. The objective is to reach general conclusions about these cases, conclusions that will hold for future cases.

From a statistical perspective, the spreadsheet represents a sample of cases. The classical idealized sampling model expects that these cases are randomly drawn from some larger group, a population. In the future, new cases will also be drawn randomly from the same population. Cases need not have unique measurements; two cases can be identical. Figure 2.1 illustrates the random sampling view of data.

This world view is very helpful in evaluating hypotheses and experimental procedures. It allows us to generalize from one sample to other samples. A sample is representative because it is randomly chosen from the same larger group that contains future samples. The sample cannot be biased by picking only cases of a certain preconceived type.

Results can be compared with the random differences that are expected in different samples.

2.1.1 Classical Statistical Comparison and Evaluation

The most widely applied evaluation technique is *hypothesis testing*, the method used to evaluate results of polls and medical studies. Hypothesis testing may be just another chapter in a fat statistics book, but it is a key concept because its theoretical foundation is so much stronger than other techniques. For large samples—and typical data-mining samples are statistically huge—the validity of the principles of statistical hypothesis testing are unassailable.

We should all be quite familiar with the concepts of a mean and variance. These are the original dimensionality-reduction techniques for summarizing a sample of cases. Our intuition should be quite comfortable with the concepts of an average value, *mean*, or the average (squared) difference from the mean, *variance*. Using just these measures is not adequate for prediction. A key piece of information is missing, the shape of the curve representing the probability of values occurring in the population. Unless a predefined probability curve can be superimposed over the population, prediction and generalization are guesswork. Sure, the population can be hypothesized to be a normally distributed bell-shape, but this is strictly surmise. Although not directly stated in these terms, a critical goal of prediction is to estimate the shape of the population curve from the sample data. This is an estimation problem much more complex than estimating a single mean or variance.

For large samples, in one important situation it is known in advance that the distribution is normal. While the distribution of the values in the sample may not be normal, the distribution of the mean of this sample and the means of other independently drawn samples is normal. This is the key result that is used in hypothesis testing. The objective is to project from the mean of the given sample to means of other samples as in Figure 2.2. Relative to a sample mean, we now have all the tools for this projection. Here our population is the means of other samples of the same size, which is called a *sampling distribution*. The initial sample mean is an unbiased estimate of the population mean. The variance from the mean is var/n, where var is the sample variance and n is the

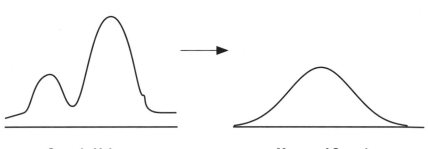

Sample Values   **Means of Samples**

Figure 2.2: Distribution of Values vs. Distribution of Sample Means

number of cases in the sample. The square root of this sampling variance is called the *standard error, se*. The population of sample means is normally distributed, and we can expect that any observed sample mean will not vary plus or minus two standard errors 95% of the time for future samples. When a poll is taken, this is the basis for reports in the media concluding that people prefer A over B with a margin of error of plus or minus 4%. With very large samples, the number of cases differing from the mean by more than two standard errors may still be large. To detect deviations from the norm, a threshold considerably higher than two standard errors may be more reasonable, and it can be selected based on the observed frequency of accurate detection.

In scientific investigations, competitive hypotheses are usually evaluated by making binary comparisons, typically good guys versus bad guys. Is A better than B? This decision is mapped into a comparison of means. The question is whether the difference in mean(A) versus mean(B) can be attributed to chance and the inherent variability of samples. Two independent samples are taken, one for A and one for B. The mean of the same feature is compared on both samples. For example, consider the efficacy of a blood pressure drug. One group of patients is given the drug, and one is not. The mean blood pressure is measured for each group to determine whether the difference in means is significant: Is $|mean(A) - mean(B)|$ greater than two standard errors?

The sampling distribution for the difference of two sample means is normally distributed. Because the two groups are independently sampled disjoint sets of cases, the variance of the difference in means is just the sum of variances. Projecting to the standard error, se, we have the significance test of Equations 2.1 and 2.2 determined from sample A with n_1 cases and sample B with n_2 cases. Significance is measured in terms of number of standard errors, sig, typically 2.

$$se(A - B) = \sqrt{\frac{var(A)}{n_1} + \frac{var(B)}{n_2}} \qquad (2.1)$$

$$\frac{|mean(A) - mean(B)|}{se(A - B)} > sig \qquad (2.2)$$

The hypothesis-testing model tells us whether differences in two hypotheses can be attributed to chance. The model is applicable when the evaluation can be reduced to comparing two means. The prediction problem is usually much too complex for this model, but comparisons of predictive performance can usually be made by the hypothesis-testing model. The performance of most prediction methods can be described in terms of a single quantity, like an error rate, that is a mean value. If we are asked to demonstrate why one solution is better than another, we can apply the hypothesis-testing model with the variations discussed in Section 2.3.

Equation 2.2 gives us the formal tools to make comparisons relative to chance. The significance of results is strongly affected by sample size. Given a difference between means, the larger the sample, the less likely the difference is due to chance. If a coin is flipped 10 times, we should not be surprised to see 6 heads. If the coin is flipped 10,000 times, a total 6,000 heads is extremely unlikely. If 6,000 heads are observed, the coin is very likely biased toward heads.

This is the central message of significance and hypothesis testing for big data. If there is a difference in means, it is very likely to be statistically significant and not due to chance. However, if there is the slightest bias in the way the data were collected, a significant difference may be illusory for new cases.

2.2   It's Big but Is It Biased?

Access to big data has challenged the thinking of scientific investigators. The issues in the debate about *outcomes analysis* reveal the same philosophical differences between statisticians and proponents of new prediction methods. Traditional scientific researchers, particularly medical researchers, insist on the most rigorous scientific experiments. They must eliminate any source of bias in the data. They usually expect modest numbers of cases. If they are testing a new drug, they cannot afford to test on thousands of patients. The conclusions of these studies will rise or fall on the basis of significance testing. If the results pass a significance test, another experiment is initiated by different researchers trying to replicate the results.

Many traditional scientific investigators are startled by the data revolution, where, for example, the records of patients are now kept in digital form. It's a relatively low cost experiment to examine the outcomes of various diagnostic tests or treatments for these patients. With so much data, significance testing is much stronger. Traditionalists will argue that there are no controls on these data, they may be biased, and therefore conclusions based on them may be invalid.

We will not settle this debate over little data with pristine experimental conditions, or big data with potentially weaker controls. If we use classical scientific methods as a gold standard, we can consider how well the large data files typically found in commercial enterprises are likely to compare to the traditional standard.

2.2.1   Objective Versus Survey Data

For a random-sample model, big data are better. They make it much less likely that an observed difference is due to chance. A potential criticism of warehoused data is that they may be of poor quality. In some instances this criticism may be valid; however, operational data are cleansed before they are placed in the data warehouse. In general, a data warehouse contains objective data, representing actual values or summaries of real transactions that are recorded online, untampered with by human hands.

In many respects these data are superior to those used in well-publicized scientific or commercial polling studies. We may not quibble

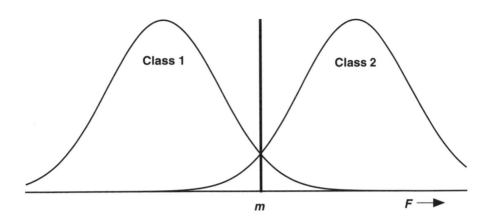

Figure 2.3: Separating Two Classes Using Means

with the data for small double-blind studies, but the data used in the larger studies are often from surveys. Such data, from questionnaires or from interviews, can be quite unreliable because answers, or even questions, may be inaccurate or misleading. Moreover, there are dangers lurking in the nonrandomness of the sample when people volunteer to participate or decline to participate. Transactional data gathered without human intervention are usually objective data. Overall, data found in a data warehouse may be of high quality and may be unbiased relative to the organization that owns the data.

2.2.2 Significance and Predictive Value

While many comparisons of results are made during data mining, our central objective is prediction, which goes far beyond determining a difference between two hypotheses. Prediction sets a much higher standard for reaching a conclusion. Consider a two-class problem with one feature. Given a new case, the problem is to determine the class of the case. Figure 2.3 is an idealized example, where each class is represented by a distinct normal curve for the single measured feature, F. In this example, it looks like it is easy to separate the two groups. The means

	Predicted Class 1	Predicted Class 2
Actual Class 1	A = 20	B = 80
Actual Class 2	C = 10	D = 9,990

Table 2.1: Standard 2×2 Confusion Table

are far apart and we might just choose to separate the two classes by $F > m$, where m is the midpoint value between the two means.

In the real world, there are a number of problems with this idealized answer. Yes, the means are different. But we cannot conclude that a case belongs to a class using just mean and variance information. There are two other factors that must be considered:

- The curve may not be normal.

- Even if the means are different, when one class is much larger than the other, the larger class may have more cases at the tails of the curve.

Consider the example of Table 2.1 for the same two-class problem. Without any search for patterns, the maximum likelihood strategy is to select the largest class. To learn from the data, a solution must be found such that the odds are greater than 50/50 for the smaller class 1. In this example, class 1 has 100 cases, and class 2 has 10,000. Only 100 errors are made by always saying class 2. An answer that gives the results of Table 2.1 would do better than chance because when it says class 1, the odds are 2 to 1 in its favor.

This tabular representation is particularly informative relative to real applications. When the sample size is increased, and the same relative ratios are maintained, statistical significance increases and the means are considered different. However, the predictive ratios A/C or D/B are unchanged, and we are no closer to making better decisions.

2.2.2.1   Too Many Comparisons?

Hypothesis testing is fundamental to many scientific investigations. If the studies are performed in one location by a principal investigator, the results are not fully accepted until they are replicated by other investigators. Replication is particularly important when the sample is relatively small. With big data, it is easy to obtain another sample that is distinct—for example, a sample from a different geographical region, which can be used to validate and replicate results.

Sometimes the same samples are used for many comparisons. For example, in comparing two populations, those who have heart attacks and those who do not, we might consider many factors, such as age, sex, weight or diet. For each factor, pairwise comparisons are made to determine significance of any differences in means. While it is common practice to determine and report significance of multiple factors in this manner, it is not surprising to see some factors called significant when they are not. We cannot be sure that the factors are completely independent. Despite the 95% confidence suggested by each pairwise comparison, when many comparisons are made, an unusual result is more likely to occur than is implied by the single confidence level. Remember the statistical puzzle from freshman statistics? How many people must be in a room to make the odds greater than 50/50 that at least two people have the same birthday? We are all surprised that it takes only 23. If too many comparisons are made, too many evaluations using the same data, we are far more likely to find an anomaly and fool ourselves with optimistic conclusions.

2.3   Classical Types of Statistical Prediction

The methods used to learn from data can vary from simple to complex, but results should be evaluated in the same way. We may have preferences in interpretation or style of solution, and these can be taken into account when selecting the best solution. Summarizing measurements of performance are needed, which are easy to compare and make sense over most applications. Two types of measurements are encountered in most evaluations of error. These evaluation criteria have been studied extensively in the research literature, and are the ones that we consider next.

2.3.1   Predicting True-or-False: Classification

Classification is the most common application of computer-based prediction. The typical problem is to distinguish between two classes, the good guys versus the bad guys: for example, businesses that will repay loans versus businesses that will default.

2.3.1.1   Error Rates

Classification is a simple true-or-false prediction. The problem can be generalized to more than two classes, but only one class can be true for a single case. Performance is measured by keeping track of the number of mistakes that are made on sample cases. The sample error rate, *erate*, described in Equation 2.3, is the percent of classifications that are incorrect. To do better than chance, we must do better than always selecting the largest class.

$$erate = \frac{errors}{cases} \tag{2.3}$$

There are many variations of the error rate that take into account additional factors such as the cost or risk of error. For example, in Table 2.1, there are two groups of errors for the usual classification problem, false positives and false negatives. We could overweight one type of error by assigning costs, $cost_{ij}$, relative to the error of misclassifying a class i case as class j.

The fundamental principle is to measure performance in terms of true-or-false classifications. Results are summarized by error rates or, if preferred, accuracy rates.

2.3.2   Forecasting Numbers: Regression

Regression, also known as *function approximation*, is the second major prediction task that requires a measure of performance. The objective is to predict a number. These are real or ordered numbers, not categories and labels. A regression prediction is usually more difficult than a classification prediction, presenting an incentive to formulate problems as classification problems whenever possible. However, for many problems, such as predicting profit or loss, the regression formulation is indispensable.

2.3.2.1 Distance Measures

The objective of regression is to minimize the distance between the true value for case i, y_i, and the predicted value y_i'. Two measures of distance are commonly used. The classical regression measure is *mse* in Equation 2.4, the mean squared error between y_i and y_i'. The *mad*, mean absolute distance, of Equation 2.5 is the more intuitive measure and is less sensitive to outliers. The square root of the *mse* in Equation 2.4, *rmse*, is usually slightly larger than the *mad*. To do better than chance, results must be better than those for always selecting the mean or median value of y.

$$mse = \frac{1}{n}\sum_{i=1}^{n}(y_i - y_i')^2 \qquad (2.4)$$

$$mad = \frac{1}{n}\sum_{i=1}^{n}|y_i - y_i'| \qquad (2.5)$$

The mean absolute distance of Equation 2.5 is analogous to the error rates used for classification. It is a measure of the average error of prediction for each y_i over n cases. If all predicted values are limited to 0 for false and 1 for true, the regression measurements are the same as classification error rates for a two-class problem. However, when the predicted values range over larger numbers, the measurements of error distance for regression diverge greatly from classification error rates. For regression, a large error in prediction is much more heavily weighted than a small error. For classification, there is no such distinction between errors. In some applications, the actual magnitude of errors is important, such as predicting the quarterly profits or losses of a company, but in other applications, just determining whether a business will show an increase in profit is useful.

Many variations are found on the regression theme, for example, measures that sum error distance over multiple variables as opposed to a single variable y. Regression methods can also solve classification problems by treating each class label as a separate regression task, where the true values are restricted to 0 and 1. A classification for a case is obtained by picking the label with the closest prediction to 1.

The key concept for measuring regression performance is that error is measured in terms of distance from the true value.

2.4 Measuring Predictive Performance

The ideal model randomly samples from populations and measures performance in terms of mean error, either error rates or distance. With large samples, very accurate projections of future performance can be made. Let's see whether the ideal model is effective for the evaluation of real-world solutions.

2.4.1 Independent Testing

Correct prediction on future cases is the objective. It does us no good to look at the prior answers and simply repeat them. The computer has an unlimited memory, and it has no difficulty repeating the answers of previous cases. While prediction methods may have varying representations, they are capable of summarizing all sampled cases. They learn much more from samples than just the value of a simple mean. The number of model parameters estimated can be in the thousands. In addition, most prediction methods are capable of finding many solutions of varying complexity, with the most complex solution equivalent to a perfect fit to the training cases. Clearly, if we wish to choose among competing models, the same set of cases cannot be used for both training and testing. Many prediction methods follow the paradigm of Figure 2.4, where the cases are split into two samples, one for training and one for testing.

2.4.1.1 Random Training and Testing

The classical approach to accurate evaluation is to randomly divide cases into train and test samples. With big data, this approach is most reasonable and convenient. Figure 2.5 illustrates this technique. Most of the cases can be used for training. Keep several thousand cases or more for testing.

The prediction method is free to examine the training data and maneuver in any way. The prediction method has no access to the test data. From the perspective of evaluation, the prediction method is a black

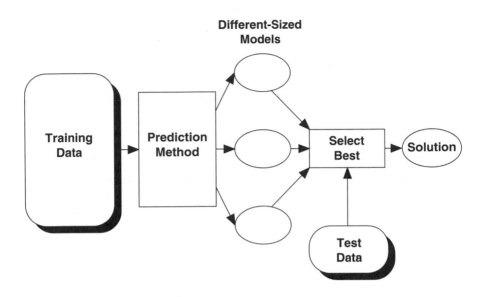

Figure 2.4: Fitting the Right-Size Model to Data

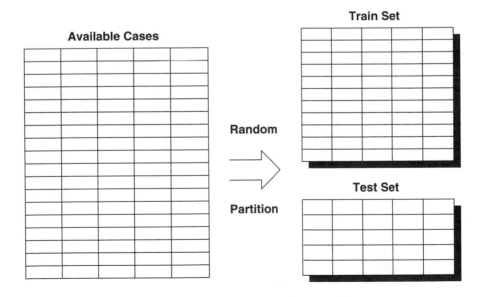

Figure 2.5: Random Train/Test Model

box. Once it finds its solution based on a sample of training cases, we can evaluate it in a fair and accurate way by measuring its mean error performance on a second sample of test data. Mean performance on test cases is an unbiased estimate of future performance on new cases.

2.4.1.2 How Accurate Is the Error Estimate?

For the ideal model, performance is measured in terms of mean errors on sample test cases. Sampling distributions of means are normally distributed, and it's easy to specify the standard error in Equation 2.6. The simplified form of Equation 2.7 can be used for classification error rates, where *merr* is the error rate. Technically, the error rate for classification is a proportion, but in large samples the error rate is equivalent to a mean. For regression, we extrapolate this analysis of sample mean error and variance and obtain Equation 2.8, where *merr* is the mean error measure, either *mad* or *mse*, and err_i is the error distance for case i, either $|y_i - y_i'|$ or $(y_i - y_i')^2$.

$$standard\ error = \sqrt{\frac{variance}{n}} \qquad (2.6)$$

$$variance = merr * (1 - merr) \qquad (2.7)$$

$$variance = \frac{1}{n} \sum_{i=1}^{n} (err_i - merr)^2 \qquad (2.8)$$

The error on new samples is expected to be within two standard errors about 95% of the time. This follows from the normal sampling distributions of means with large samples. This expectation is slightly weaker for the *mse* measure of error, where the mean is already a squared number.

The standard error has a number of practical uses:

- It indicates how widely the performance can vary under ideal random sampling conditions. This corresponds to the contribution of chance.

- It implies guidelines on the number of test cases that should be set aside to reduce chance variation. We decide how much random variation we can tolerate.

- The standard error is a useful heuristic for comparing two solutions and specifying preferences. For example, we may prefer
  a simpler solution that is close (within one standard error) to a
  better-performing but more complex solution. The standard error
  helps measure this closeness factor.

For large test samples, numbering in the thousands, we can expect
the variation of estimates to be quite small. Where rare events are of
particular importance, the test sample size must be increased beyond
the expected size suggested by the standard error to allow for adequate
testing in a low-prevalence environment.

2.4.1.3 Comparing Results for Error Measures

Performance is measured in terms of mean error on independent test
cases, the error rate for classification and either the *mad* or *mse* for
regression. To compare two results—for example, the results for two
different prediction methods—the standard hypothesis-testing model of
Equations 2.9 and 2.10 can determine whether differences between
$merr(A)$ and $merr(B)$ are significant. Typically, *sig* is set to 2, and if
the inequality in Equation 2.10 is satisfied, the difference is considered
significant.

$$se(A - B) = \sqrt{\frac{var(A)}{n_1} + \frac{var(B)}{n_2}} \qquad (2.9)$$

$$\frac{|merr(A) - merr(B)|}{se(A - B)} > sig \qquad (2.10)$$

Given the mean error, *merr*, independently compute the standard
errors for each of the two compared methods. For classification problems
and error rates, the computation is trivial because the standard error
can be computed directly from *merr*. While the math is very simple,
there is a sometimes onerous data requirement: two independent test
sets are required. Method A is tested on test set A; method B is tested
on test set B. This significance test is statistically accurate, and independently drawn random samples are eminently fair. Still, separate testing
disturbs our democratic sense of fair play. We can easily improve our
intuitive position by using two test sets with equal numbers of cases. If

feasible, we also test method A on test set B, and test method B on test set A, averaging the results from both significance tests.

The advent of big data and data mining makes it more likely that we can splurge on two test sets. Using only one test set, the analysis is trickier, requiring a case-by-case, pairwise comparison. This is somewhat inconvenient because different methods may produce case results in different formats, and the results of two methods must be paired case by case even for the classification error rate. For publication, accurate significance testing is done by examining paired case results. In practice, comparisons are often done heuristically. The standard error of each *merr* is computed, and the larger of the two is used for the joint standard error, $se(A - B)$. This maximum *se* heuristic approach is particularly enticing when we have big data and expect most small differences to be significant.

For a single test set, the joint variance, $var(A - B)$, is correctly estimated by a paired case-by-case computation. The compared methods are often correlated, typically giving similar answers on most cases. A significance test should emphasize only those cases where the methods give different results. Equations 2.11, 2.12 and 2.13 are the computations necessary for the single test set significance test, where $merr(A - B)$ is the difference in mean error, $merr(A) - merr(B)$. $Err(A - B)_i$ is the difference in error for A and B on case i, $Err(A)_i - Err(B)_i$. *Merr* is one of the three error measures: *erate*, *mse* and *mad*. The appropriate measure is used to compute the error. For example, using *mad*, if the true answer for a case is 5, and method A says 3, and method B says 6, then $Err(A - B) = |3 - 5| - |6 - 5| = 1$. For classification error rates, a case error is assigned 1, and a correct classification is assigned a 0. For example, if method A is correct, but method B makes an error on case i, then $Err(A - B)_i = 0 - 1 = -1$. Thus, for classification error rates, only differences in answers from A and B contribute to the variance.

$$var(A - B) = \frac{1}{n} \sum_{i=1}^{n} (err(A - B)_i - merr(A - B))^2 \qquad (2.11)$$

$$se(A - B) = \sqrt{\frac{var(A - B)}{n}} \qquad (2.12)$$

$$\frac{|merr(A) - merr(B)|}{se(A - B)} > sig \qquad (2.13)$$

The standard errors for the one or two test set models are not the same. If we consider a medical treatment metaphor, with two independent test sets, we are testing one treatment on one group of patients, and another treatment, usually a placebo, on a different group. This is quite typical in medical science. For a single test set, we test both treatments on all patients, and then compare results. The latter scenario is less likely in medical science, but much more likely in data mining. Both models are correct, but represent different sampling scenarios. Mathematically, the variance for the difference in means can be written in terms of the independent variances minus a correlation factor. When the correlation between the means is very high—for example, comparing two classifiers that behave similarly on the cases—then the standard error, $se(A - B)$, is small. A high correlation is typical of many comparisons of prediction methods, making it even more likely that significant differences will be found. This correlation is the rationale for expecting the maximum single *se* heuristic to be a conservative standard on real-world comparisons.

2.4.1.4 Ideal or Real-World Sampling?

As long as the original data are representative of future data, the ideal random sampling model, with evaluation on independent test data, is very accurate. The net result of the evaluation is a specific estimate of future performance in terms of average expected error.

Scientific experimenters try at all costs to conform to the ideal model. Even then other researchers sometimes find bias in the data or the experimental procedures. Obviously, we try to do as much as possible to alleviate potential problems with the data or the mining procedures. There are many ways in which data can be contaminated, and careful data preparation is the main defense against contamination. For example, random training and testing may not be accurate when the original sample contains cases that are related or duplicated, such as multiple episodes of a service call to the same customer. Some potential problems can be detected during data mining. The logic prediction methods, such as decision trees or rules, are particularly helpful in detecting data problems. They present their solutions in simple comparative tests, such as *age* > 30, that allow us to ask whether the answer makes sense or is traceable to poor samples.

Whenever a very simple solution performs extremely well, we must question whether the data are poorly formed. It may very well be that gold has been mined, but the alternatives must be considered. For example, the prediction methods expect a spreadsheet data model with the goals labeled as special, distinct features that cannot be used in a solution. Occasionally, there are other features that act as surrogates and pose a form of circular reasoning for the labeled features. This may be obvious when the solution is revealed, or a subtle problem is present that is recognized by a specialist in the application area. The key message is to be cautious about simple, highly accurate answers—for example, a decision tree with only a few nodes, which makes few errors.

If the answer is extremely complex, and gives very strong results, we must also be cautious about the test data, particularly if the training data and test data were divided by random sampling. The main worry is that there is some form of case duplication in the samples, with nearly identical cases in both the training and test sets. Detecting this type of problem is subtle. To get good results, the training cases are expected to be similar to the test cases. Once again the logic methods are helpful in examining the samples. When very narrow ranges on real-valued variables are observed with extremely good results, we must be concerned about duplication. For example, a decision-tree solution with many rules of the form "length of time in business = 8.5 to 9.5 years" or "length of time in business = 10 to 11 years" should concern us, when we expect that there is no particular reason for such a fine distinction in groupings.

Overall, it's not easy to spot these sampling problems. In many scientific fields, researchers wait for their experimental results to be replicated by others. If it is known that a factor such as geography will not influence results, then it can be worthwhile to use all cases from a particular geographic area as a distinct test set, and those from the other areas as training data. This approximates the scientific replication but we must worry whether the populations are different. These nonrandom divisions of data still maintain independence of test data, but they require detailed knowledge of the application. There is one additional factor that is highly influential in real-world application and will often affect the division of data into training and test cases. We consider the time factor next.

2.4.1.5 *Training and Testing from Different Time Periods*

For many real-world applications, a major assumption of the ideal model, sampling from a stationary population, is violated. The population may be nonstationary; it may change over time. If these changes are slight, the ideal sampling model can still be effective. Most prediction methods can vary the complexity of their solutions. They have a closet full of shoes of different sizes, and they try the shoes on the data until they find the right size. In the research literature, much attention has been given to getting a perfect fit, usually to not overfit the data. Overfitting is a particular concern because modern prediction methods are capable of finding solutions that cover without error all cases in a training sample. Solutions overfit when they are tailored too closely to a sample whose characteristics will vary for future cases. The perfect fit is measured on future cases. If the data are representative and will not change much, then the perfect fit is the correct answer for future application. If the data are expected to change, then we are usually better off slightly underfitting, choosing a somewhat simpler, less variable solution. For the ideal model, this would be considered a pessimistic bias. With a changing population, it may be wise to leave extra room to fit in the shoe.

We cannot know how the future population may change. With a nonstationary population, more should be done to spot trends in the data. From an evaluation perspective, it is wise to organize the training and test data as in Figure 2.6. The training cases are taken from a period prior to a specified time, and the test cases are taken from the following period. The length of the time periods depends on knowledge of the application. This model maintains two samples: the training cases are independent of the test cases. In exchange for no longer viewing the cases as random samples from the same population, we now have an ironclad separation between the train and test samples. Because the samples may change with time, we have a closer simulation of the task of prediction: train from the current period to predict for a future period.

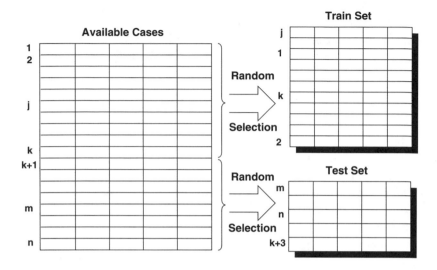

Figure 2.6: Train/Test Procedure for Nonstationary Populations

The time-dependencies among the cases may be very strong, so strong that they are considered a *time series* where the cases must keep a sequential order in time. This sequential order of cases allows for modeling trends in the data. For example, the data may be records of the weekly sales of a product, and the objective is to predict future sales or perhaps whether sales will rise or fall. Figure 2.7 illustrates this type of data organization for evaluation. In Chapter 3, we will consider transformations of time-series data from the strict dependencies of Figure 2.7 into the simpler and more amenable analytical model of Figure 2.6.

In summary, for time-dependent data, it is advantageous to employ the evaluation model of Figure 2.6. Training cases and test cases should be allotted from different time periods, with the test cases coming from the most recent period.

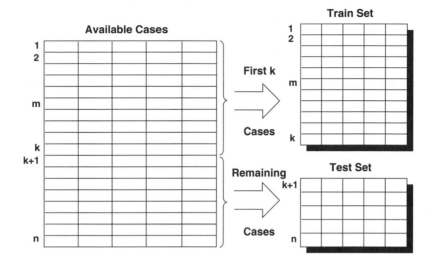

Figure 2.7: Train/Test Procedure for Time-Series Data

2.5 Too Much Searching and Testing?

We have reduced the problem of evaluation to a mean measure of performance on independent test cases. The value of this measure is an unbiased estimate of the future performance of a proposed solution. Under ideal sampling conditions on large numbers of test cases, future performance will be very close to this measure.

In mining data, we need to do more than get an estimate of future performance. Comparisons of alternative solutions or alternative approaches will be made, and we must decide which of these alternatives are best. Some examples of the performance factors that should be compared include the following:

- Variable complexity solutions

- Data-mining program parameters

- Data smoothing and feature selection

Most decisions can be made by pairwise comparison of error. Is solution A better than solution B? Does the prediction method do better with feature selection or without? The formal procedure for making such a comparison is a significance test on these competing hypotheses. Because we have big data, with lots of test cases, we informally know that slight differences will be significant and not due to chance. If we have one test set, or even two, we must wonder how many times we can draw from the same well? The more comparisons that are made, the more likely that the absolute best-performing approach was not taken. While this is of concern to those who insist on completely unbiased estimates of future performance, we can expect to make effective comparisons and get valid estimates when the evaluation is done fairly, and the candidates for evaluation are based on reasonable training protocols.

The test data must be independent of the training data, and reserved for testing and not training. Serious blunders in evaluation were made by early researchers in pattern recognition when they used test data incrementally during training to help make decisions about alternatives. They allowed the test data to overrule decisions that were clearly better from the training data view, but were weaker from the test data. In a modern approach, a wall is erected between the training and test cases. Evaluation takes place after complete solutions are found. If a prediction method searches and enumerates vast numbers of solutions, saves them and then evaluates each solution on the test data, the conclusions would be highly biased, still resembling training on test cases. But when the prediction method is restricted to finding solutions that are best when only the training data are examined, then the testing results are valid.

The question of how much the test data can be used is of major strategic importance in data mining. It is critical to balance the use of test data for fairness in evaluation with finding effective solutions. Yes, when we publish, we are the saints who have removed all bias from the experiments. If we want to solve a practical problem, we maximize the overall effectiveness of data mining, perhaps at the expense of a potential mistake. In practice, the risks are minimal with large test samples when a few practical guidelines are followed:

- Perform the evaluation on a completed solution. Training should be based on minimizing an error measure for the training cases.

- The prediction methods should generate different solutions based on varying global parameters. Avoid solutions that locally override training solutions for improved test results.

Among the general categories of relatively safe multiple-evaluation techniques are multiple-complexity fit solutions, such as training and evaluating neural nets of different sizes or pruning a decision tree based on significance testing at different thresholds on the training data. Tuning parameters in a program are relatively safe, too, when they affect the global style of generating solutions and are applied only to the training data. The methods of Chapter 4, that smooth data or select features based on training data, are generally quite safe and do not bias the evaluation. An example of a risky technique is pruning selected parts of a solution that test poorly on the test data. This potentially biases performance estimates.

Yes, it would be best to avoid multiple testing of error on test cases. In practice, we have many decisions to make about the best way to proceed for data mining. If we are judicious in our use of training and test data, we can do multiple comparisons and still maintain relatively reliable estimates of future performance.

2.6 Why Are Errors Made?

When predictive performance is measured as mean error on sample cases, error can be decomposed into the subcomponents of Equation 2.14. A solution proposed by a prediction method can do no better than the best solution. The best solution is the one that minimizes test error, and the minimum error may be greater than zero. For example, a case can have identical measurements with two different true answers, or the features themselves may be weak predictors.

$$error = best + bias + variance \qquad (2.14)$$

Two factors, bias and variance, contribute to performance less than the best possible. With unlimited data, the bias of a proposed solution is the difference in error between the best solution and the proposed solution. For finite random samples, bias is also the difference in error between the best solution and the average of proposed solutions found for many samples of the same size. Variance is the expected difference in error between a solution found for a single sample and the average solution obtained over many random samples.

How good are the results obtained by measuring mean error on n independent test cases? The best result is obtained by testing on an extremely large test set, representing the full population. The test sample result is an unbiased estimate: the average estimate of many smaller samples of size n is the same as pooling and testing on all samples. The variance of the mean error estimated from a single random test sample has already been described, and is relatively small for a test sample numbering in the thousands of cases. Thus, the estimates of performance on several thousand independent test cases can be close to best, with no bias and little variance.

The effective evaluation of solutions is essential for data mining, but it does not guarantee that proposed solutions are very good. Ideally, the training error of a solution should be close to the test error. Poor performance or disparities between training error and test error can be decomposed into the same three factors that comprise mean error. The floor on performance is the error of the best solution. If the features are of poor quality, that alone will produce a high error for the best solution. A prediction method has no control over the quality of the features and must accept this source of error. Its mission is to find the best solution. Two obstacles remain to meet this goal: bias and variance. A solution may be biased and incapable of producing the same results as the best solution. The second source of error is the variance of a single-sample solution from solutions found on different samples.

In the classical model of prediction from data, a single random sample is presented for training, and the goal is to find a single solution. Some prediction methods, like decision trees or neural nets, examine many solutions of different sizes. The most complex solution may fit the training data with no error. Complex solutions may have little bias, and with unlimited data, they get the correct answer. However, these complex solutions vary greatly from sample to sample. A solution found for one sample may not do nearly as well on a second sample. Other prediction methods, like linear methods, have low variance but high bias. They have restricted representations, producing simple solutions that are similar for all samples, and may have substantial error on the training cases. Modern prediction methods try to minimize error by proposing solutions of different complexities, choosing the one that minimizes test error, a trade-off of complexity (low bias) and simplicity (low variance). Simple solutions do not vary much from sample to sample, but they may be biased and incapable of solving problems that require complex solutions. Instead of selecting a single solution, some prediction methods may reduce variance and improve predictive performance by averaging or voting answers from several complex solutions. The practical application of these concepts to data mining is discussed in upcoming chapters.

2.7 Bibliographic and Historical Remarks

Hypothesis testing is a foundation of modern experimental science. A description of techniques for evaluating significant differences in two means can be found in any applied statistics primer. Traditional texts focus on small samples, at least by data-mining expectations, and their exposition is complete with caveats on the applicability of assumptions with correction factors, such as the t-test. With big data, the mathematical principles of probability, the law of large numbers and the central limit theorem are seen in their full glory with straightforward application to test data.

A perspective on the evolution of statistical models and their common bonds with data mining is given in [Elder and Pregibon, 1996]. One of the key advances in statistics since the advent of the computer age is evaluation by resampling, that is, repeated random training and testing on a single sample. Big data makes this important topic less relevant. An extensive presentation and justification of the use of test cases for evaluation in classification and regression is given in the CART book [Breiman, Friedman, Olshen and Stone, 1984].

The conflicting views of statisticians on the role of big data and "outcomes analysis" in medical science are described in [Kolata, 1994]. The importance of modeling the most recent period for practical applications for time-dependent data is illustrated in [Makridakis et al., 1993].

3

Preparing the Data

Data-mining research has emphasized prediction methods or database organization. The preparation of data is sometimes dismissed as a topic too mundane for extensive research. In the real world of data-mining applications, the situation is reversed. More effort is expended preparing data than applying a prediction program to data.

Rejecting the view that data preparation is more than specialized "one-shot" programs, we face the daunting task of generalizing knowledge that is often application dependent. Prediction programs look at data in a mechanical way. They expect the data to be specified in a *standard form*. Given this form, they search a space of possibilities in a very comprehensive way, far exceeding human capabilities. But they are at the mercy of the original data descriptions that constrain the potential quality of solutions.

Prediction methods are quite capable of finding valuable patterns in data. It is straightforward to apply a method to data and then judge the value of its results based on the estimated predictive performance. This does not diminish the role of careful attention to data preparation. While the prediction methods may have very strong theoretical capabilities, in practice all these methods may be limited by a shortage of data relative to the unlimited space of possibilities that they may search. This is true even for big data. The prediction methods will benefit from any insight into the problem that leads to a revised and improved set of features. For example, the simple specification of an important ratio can lead to improved predictive results. To a large extent, the design and organization of data, including the setting of goals and the composition of features, is done by humans.

There are two central goals for the preparation of data:

- To organize data into a standard form that is ready for processing by prediction programs.

- To prepare features that lead to the best predictive performance.

It's easy to specify a standard form that is compatible with most prediction methods. It's much harder to generalize concepts for composing the most predictive features.

3.1   A Standard Form

The concept of a standard form is more than simple formatting of data. A standard form helps to understand the advantages and limitations of different prediction techniques and how they reason with data. The standard form model of data constrains our world view. To find the best set of features, it is important to examine the types of features that fit this model of data, so that they may be manipulated to increase predictive performance.

Most prediction methods require that data be in a standard form with standard types of measurements. The features must be encoded in a numerical format such as binary true-or-false features, numerical features, or possibly numeric codes. In addition, for classification, a clear goal must be specified. While some databases may readily be arranged in standard form, many others may be combinations of numerical fields or text, with thousands of possibilities for each data field, and multiple instances of the same field specification.

Prediction methods may differ greatly, but they share a common perspective. Their view of the world is cases organized in a spreadsheet format. Table 3.1 illustrates this general organization, where a row C_i is the i-th case, and column entries are values of measurements, $V_{i,j}$, for the j-th feature f_j. For example, a bank's business loan records could be organized in this format. If row 1 is the case of company XYZ, and column 1 is the feature "Number of years in business," then the entry for the intersection of row 1 and column 1, $V_{1,1}$, is the number of years that company XYZ has been in business.

Case	f_1	$\cdots$	f_k
C_1	$V_{1,1}$	$\cdots$	$V_{1,k}$
$\cdots$	$\cdots$	$\cdots$	$\cdots$
C_i	$V_{i,1}$	$\cdots$	$V_{i,k}$
$\cdots$	$\cdots$	$\cdots$	$\cdots$
C_n	$V_{n,1}$	$\cdots$	$V_{n,k}$

Table 3.1: Spreadsheet Data Format

3.1.1 Standard Measurements

The spreadsheet format becomes a standard form when the features are restricted to certain types. Individual measurements for cases must conform to the specified feature type. There are two standard feature types; both are encoded in a numerical format, so that all values, $V_{i,j}$, are numbers.

- True-or-false variables: These values are encoded as 1 for true and 0 for false. For example, feature j is assigned 1 if the business is current in supplier payments and 0 if not.

- Ordered variables: These are numerical measurements where the order is important, and X > Y has meaning. A variable could be a naturally occurring, real-valued measurement such as the number of years in business, or it could be an artificial measurement such as an index reflecting the banker's subjective assessment of the chances that a business plan may fail.

A true-or-false variable describes an event where one of two mutually exclusive events occurs. Some events have more than two possibilities. For example, the color of a car could be coded as a single value selected from a code sheet of many mutually exclusive colors. Such a code, sometimes called a *categorical* variable, could be represented as a single number. In standard form, a categorical variable is represented as m individual true-or-false variables, where m is the number of possible values for the code.

While databases are sometimes accessible in spreadsheet format, or can readily be converted into this format, they often may not be easily mapped into standard form. Examples of difficulties in mapping data into standard form are the following raw data types:

- Free text

- Replicated fields: multiple instances of the same feature recorded in different data fields

Mapping raw data into features and measurements is more than a straightforward mechanical process. The transformation represents a general conceptual model that is applicable across a broad group of prediction methods. In Chapter 5, prediction methods will be described that find several distinct types of solutions:

- Math, such as linear discriminants and neural nets that use arithmetic operations

- Logic, such as decision trees or rules that compute in terms of true or false

- Distance, such as nearest-neighbor methods that measure case similarity

Depending on the type of solution, a prediction method may have a clear preference for either true-or-false or ordered features. In addition to prediction methods, supplementary techniques work with the same prepared data to select an interesting subset of features. Some of these techniques summarize features using means and variances, transformations that are effective for both ordered and true-or-false features. Many methods readily reason with ordered numerical variables. Difficulties may arise with unordered numerical variables, the categorical features. Because a specific code is arbitrary, it is not suitable for many prediction methods. For example, a math method cannot compute appropriate weights or means based on a set of arbitrary codes. A distance method cannot effectively compute distance based on arbitrary codes. While many logic methods may process codes without a transformation into multiple binary codes, many methods—for example, binary-tree induction—will implicitly make this transformation. Other logic methods may require that all features be categorical. Techniques for transforming ordered numerical features into sets of true-or-false variables are discussed in Sections 4.5.1 and 4.5.1.3.

Case	f_1	$\cdots$	f_k	G
C_1	$V_{1,1}$	$\cdots$	$V_{1,k}$	$V_{1,k+1}$
$\cdots$	$\cdots$	$\cdots$	$\cdots$	$\cdots$
C_i	$V_{i,1}$	$\cdots$	$V_{i,k}$	$V_{i,k+1}$
$\cdots$	$\cdots$	$\cdots$	$\cdots$	$\cdots$
C_n	$V_{n,1}$	$\cdots$	$V_{n,k}$	$V_{n,k+1}$

Table 3.2: Standard Form

The standard-form model is a data presentation that is uniform and effective across a wide spectrum of prediction methods and supplementary data-reduction techniques. Its model of data makes explicit the constraints faced by most prediction methods in searching for good solutions. Formulating a problem and assembling a set of features is no easy task. Constraining values to two simple numerical data types limits the possibilities, yet focuses attention on the primary task of composing an effective set of features.

3.1.2 Goals

One last bookkeeping task remains before a standard form is ready to be processed by prediction methods. A label is attached to one or more features indicating that these special features are goals, not predictors. The features designated as goals are not used in solutions. For classification, either a code or true-or-false variables are used. For regression, ordered variables are the goals. The standard spreadsheet form just prior to processing by the prediction methods looks like Table 3.2, where the last feature is labeled the goal, G.

3.2 Data Transformations

A central objective of data preparation for predictive data mining is to transform the raw data into a standard spreadsheet form. Sometimes the data in a warehouse are already in standard form, or the prediction methods work directly with a specialized data format. Sometimes it's

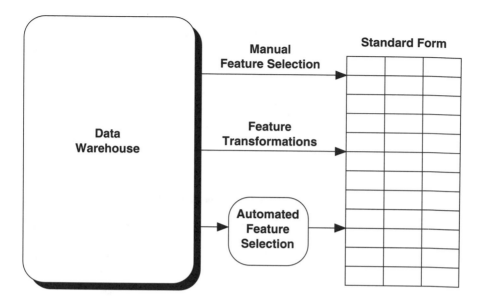

Figure 3.1: From Data Warehouse to Standard Form

just a formatting exercise to get the data into a standard spreadsheet form. In general, though, two additional tasks are associated with producing the standard-form spreadsheet:

- Feature selection

- Feature composition

Figure 3.1 illustrates these steps in the production of the standard form. Based on knowledge of the topic and the goals of the mining effort, the human analyst may select a subset of the multitude features found in the data warehouse. Once the data are in standard form, there are a number of effective automated procedures for feature selection; these will be described in Chapter 4. In terms of the standard spreadsheet form, feature selection will delete some of the features, represented by columns in the spreadsheet. Chapter 4 discusses some of the techniques for feature selection by deleting redundant and nonpredictive features. Automated feature selection is usually effective, much more so than composing and extracting new features. This implies that many decisions by the human analyst may be needed, but when in doubt, always include the extra features in the initial standard form. The computer is smart about deleting weak features, but relatively dumb in the more demanding task of composing new features or transforming raw data into more predictive forms.

Having the data resident in a data warehouse provides some structure to the data. For data mining, the data are unlikely to be signal data or image data that require very specialized feature composition. Still, in many instances, there are transformations of the data that can have a surprisingly strong impact on results for prediction methods. In this sense, the composition of the features is a greater determining factor in the quality of results than the specific prediction methods used to produce those results. In most instances, feature composition is dependent on knowledge of the application. We review next a few general types of transformations of data fields that may improve data-mining results.

3.2.1 Normalizations

Data in standard form can be processed by many prediction methods. The spreadsheet data presentation, with its rows for cases and columns for features, should lend itself to interpretation and explanation. An individual case can readily be summarized because the measured values are scaled in an expected and recognizable form. Some methods, typically math and distance methods, may need normalized data for best results. The measured values can be scaled to a specified range, for example, -1 to $+1$. For example, neural nets generally train better when the measured values are small. If they are not normalized, distance measures for nearest-neighbor methods will overweight those features that have larger values. A binary 0 or 1 value should not compute distance on the same scale as age in years. There are many ways of normalizing data. Here are two simple and effective normalization techniques:

- Decimal scaling

- Standard deviation normalization

To varying extents, normalizations degrade the interpretability of feature values. Decimal scaling moves the decimal point, but still preserves most of the original character of the value. Normalization by standard deviations often works well with distance measures, but transforms the data into a form unrecognizable from the original data. Equation 3.1 describes decimal scaling, where $v(i)$ is the value of feature v for case i. The typical scale maintains the values in a range of -1 to 1. The maximum absolute $v(i)$ is found in the training data, and then the decimal point is moved until the new, scaled maximum absolute value is less than 1. This divisor is then applied to all other $v(i)$. For example, if the largest value is 903, then the maximum value of the feature becomes .903, and the divisor for all $v(i)$ is 1,000.

$$v'(i) = \frac{v(i)}{10^k}, \quad \text{for smallest } k \text{ such that } \max(|v'(i)|) < 1 \qquad (3.1)$$

For distance methods, normalization using means and standard deviations is often effective, but is more radical in transforming the characteristics of the initial data. For a feature v, the mean value, $mean(v)$, and the standard deviation, $sd(v)$, are computed from the training data. Then for a case i, the feature value is transformed as shown in Equation 3.2.

$$v'(i) = \frac{v(i) - mean(v)}{sd(v)} \qquad (3.2)$$

Why not treat normalization as an implicit part of a prediction method? The simple answer is that normalizations are useful for several diverse prediction methods. More importantly, though, normalization is not a "one-shot" event. If a method normalizes training data, the identical normalizations must be applied to future data. The normalization parameters must be saved along with a solution. If decimal scaling is used, the divisors derived from the training data are saved for each feature. If standard-error normalizations are used, the means and standard errors for each feature are saved for application to new data.

3.2.2   Data Smoothing

A numerical feature, y, may range over many distinct values, sometimes as many as the number of training cases. In most applications, minor differences between these values are not significant and may even degrade performance. They may be considered random variations of the same underlying value. Hence, it can be advantageous to smooth the values of the variable.

To understand data smoothing, consider the regression problem. Predicting the value of an ordered variable, y, from a set of features $\mathbf{x}$ is sometimes described as a signal and noise problem. The model is extended to include the stochastic component ϵ in Equation 3.3. Thus, the true function may not produce a zero-error distance from the stored answer. In contrast to classification, where the labels are assumed to be correct, for regression the predicted y values could be explained by a number of factors including a random variation or noise component, ϵ, in the signal, y.

$$y = f(x_1 \ldots x_n) + \epsilon \qquad (3.3)$$

This formulation of the regression problem implies that practical solutions are smoothers. Regression methods try to approximate and generalize data with curves that smooth out random variations. Data smoothing can be understood as doing the same kind of smoothing on the features themselves with the same objective of removing noise in the features. From the perspective of generalization to new cases, even features that are expected to have little error in their values may benefit from smoothing of their values to reduce random variation. The primary focus of regression methods is to smooth the predicted output variable, but complex regression smoothing cannot be done for every feature in the spreadsheet. Some methods, such as neural nets with sigmoid functions, or regression trees that use the mean value of a partition, have smoothers implicit in their representation.

Smoothing the original data, particularly real-valued numerical features, may have beneficial predictive consequences. In Chapter 4, we review a number of simple data smoothers that can help predictive performance. Many simple smoothers can be specified that average similar measured values. However, our emphasis is not solely on enhancing prediction but also on reducing dimensions, reducing the number of distinct values for a feature. Reducing values is particularly useful for logic-based methods, and smoothers that are compatible with logic methods are considered in Chapter 4. These same techniques can be used to "discretize" continuous features into a set of true-or-false features, each covering a fixed range of values.

3.2.3 Differences and Ratios

We would like the prediction programs to do all the work and discover the important relationships, but the specifications of the features and goals play critical roles in predictive performance. Even small changes to features or goals can produce significant improvements in performance. The effects of relatively minor transformations of features are particularly important in the specifications of the goals. Two types of simple transformations to the specified goals, differences and ratios, sometimes produce better results than a simple goal of predicting a number.

Each of these transformations is helpful in specifying goals of some of the applications of Chapter 7. In one application, the objective is to move the controls for a manufacturing process to an optimal setting. The goal can be specified as the magnitude either of the best setting or of a move from the current position. In this application, better performance is obtained by predicting the magnitude of the move than the actual new position: predictive test results are better for a difference in setting, $s(t+1) - s(t)$, rather than the new setting at time $t+1$, $s(t+1)$. Clearly, if $s(t+1)$ is predicted, then the difference can be computed after the fact. The data for this application give us a clue that the difference might be better; the range of values for the moves is generally much smaller than the range of values for the control settings.

In the aforementioned application, using the difference produces better results, but reasonable answers can still be achieved when predicting the actual value. In a second application, however, the difference in performance for the primary alternatives is clear-cut. There, the objective is to predict future sales performance of a prescription drug for each physician. For the obvious goal of predicting the next quarter's unit prescriptions of each physician, the prediction programs do poorly. They also do poorly with predictions of net change from current prescription levels. However, when a ratio is considered, such as a net change in market share, performance is greatly improved.

The model used to represent solutions may have weaknesses that suggest directions for composing new features. For example, a logic method can readily compose A and B from the original features, but may need a new feature to determine $A < B$. Data transformations are not universally best. The lesson to be learned is that a major role remains for human insight into the problem definition. Attention should be paid to composing the features and to improving performance by reacting to experimental results. Relatively simple transformations can sometimes be far more important to performance than switching to another type of prediction method.

3.3 Missing Data

The standard form is a spreadsheet with numerical values. What happens when some data values are missing? If the label is missing, the case is generally discarded. But even with big data, the subset of cases with complete data may be relatively small. Future cases may also present themselves with missing values. Most prediction methods do not manage missing values very well; a missing value cannot be multiplied or compared.

If the missing values can be isolated to only a few features, the prediction program can find several solutions: one solution using all features, other solutions not using the features with many expected missing values. Sufficient cases may remain when rows or columns in the spreadsheet are ignored. Logic methods may have an advantage with surrogate approaches for missing values. A substitute feature is found that approximately mimics the performance of the missing feature. In effect, a subproblem is posed with a goal of predicting the missing value. The relatively complex surrogate approach is perhaps the best of a weak group of methods that compensate for missing values. The surrogate techniques are generally associated with decision trees. The most natural prediction method for missing values may be the decision rules. They can readily be induced with missing data and applied to cases with missing data because the rules are not mutually exclusive.

An obvious question is whether these missing values can be filled in during data preparation prior to the application of the prediction methods. The complexity of the surrogate approach would seem to imply that these are individual subproblems that cannot be solved by simple transformations. This is generally true. Consider the failings of some of these simple extrapolations.

- Replace all missing values with a single global constant.

- Replace a missing value with its feature mean.

- Replace a missing value with its feature and class mean.

These simple solutions are tempting. Their main flaw is that the substituted value is not the correct value. By replacing the missing feature values with a constant or a few values, the data are biased. For example, if the missing values for a feature are replaced by the feature means of the correct class, an equivalent label may have been implicitly substituted for the hidden class label. Clearly, using the label is circular, but replacing missing values with a constant will homogenize the missing value cases into a uniform subset directed toward the class label of the largest group of cases with missing values. If missing values are replaced with a single global constant for all features, an unknown value may be implicitly made into a positive factor that is not objectively justified. For example, in medicine, an expensive test may not be ordered because the diagnosis has already been confirmed. This should not lead us to always conclude that same diagnosis when this expensive test is missing.

In general, it is speculative and often misleading to replace missing values using a simple scheme of data preparation. It is best to generate multiple solutions with and without features that have missing values or to rely on prediction methods that have surrogate schemes, such as some of the logic methods.

3.4   Time-Dependent Data

The product of data preparation is a standard spreadsheet form. This model of data fits the classical sampling model, and it's easy to see the dimensions of the data in terms of cases, features and values. There is another dimension, time, that is often essential for applied data mining. Time-series problems are of particular interest in business applications, where trends are critical to forecasting future patterns.

Practical applications will range from those having strong time-dependent relationships to those with loose time relationships that mix the standard sampling model with more specialized time series. Real-world problems with time-dependencies are much more common in modern applications than might be expected from reading the data-mining literature. Approximately 50% of the applications described in Chapter 7 have time-dependencies. Once again, the standard form is invoked for data preparation, with data transformations that map high-dimensional, time-oriented data into a more manageable format. Such transformations are critical for real-world applications of data mining.

We review the classical times-series data model next, where data are highly time-dependent.

3.4.1 Time Series

Let's examine the behavior of a single feature measured over time. Instead of a single measurement at a fixed time found in a standard case, we have a series of values over fixed time units. For example, a temperature reading could be measured every hour, or the sales of a product could be recorded every day. This is the classical univariate time-series problem, where it is expected that the value of the variable at a given time is related to previous values. Figure 3.2 is an example of these measured values for a well-known univariate times series—the daily closing values, and the 200-day moving-average values of the Dow Jones Industrial Average over a period of one year from April 1995 to April 1996. The x-axis is the unit of time, and the y-axis is the measured value. The concept of a moving average is discussed later in Section 3.4.2.2. The exact units of time depend on the application, but they are sampled at fixed intervals. In Chapter 7, we consider a control application where the values are measured every 30 seconds, a communications network application where they are sampled every hour and a drug sales application where they are sampled every three months. Because the time series is measured at fixed units of time, the series of values can be expressed as $t(1), t(2), \ldots t(i), \ldots t(n)$, where $t(n)$ is the most recent value.

The sampled values of the variable can be gathered in a number of ways. They may occur naturally in this format and are therefore readily available. In other instances, raw transactions must be counted during the fixed time period. Here are some examples:

- An instrument reading is recorded every x units of time.

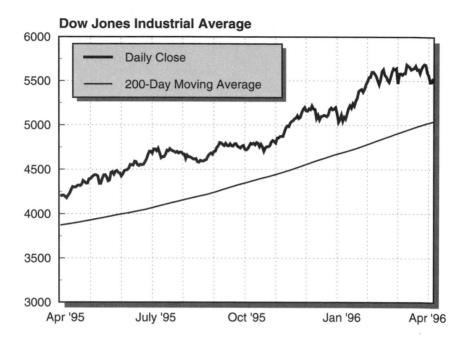

Figure 3.2: Examples of Univariate Time Series

- Sales of a product or error messages on a network are recorded as transactions. The number of transactions during a specific time interval is counted.

Sometimes the total transactional count is not as important as just determining whether the event actually occurred. For example, instead of counting the number of error messages, it may be determined whether any error occurred during a fixed interval, assigning a 1 for yes and 0 for no. Whether the data are measured readings at the exact indicated time, or counts of events that occurred between two fixed times, the net result of summarizing the variable is a series of values recorded over fixed intervals of time.

So far, a series of numbers has been described, but no goals have been established. For many problems, the most important number is the last number in the series, $t(n)$, for example, the most recent sales

$$t0 \; t1 \; t2 \; t3 \; \underbrace{t4 \; t5 \; t6 \; t7 \; t8}_{lag=5} \; t9$$

Figure 3.3: Time Series with a Window of Size 5

Case	F1	F2	F3	F4	F5	Goal
1	t0	t1	t2	t3	t4	t5
2	t1	t2	t3	t4	t5	t6
3	t2	t3	t4	t5	t6	t7
4	t3	t4	t5	t6	t7	t8
5	t4	t5	t6	t7	t8	t9

Figure 3.4: Transformation of Time Series to Standard Form

figures. The goal is to forecast $t(n + 1)$ from $t(n)$. In the simplest transformation of a time series, a case is the feature-goal pair $\{t(n-1), t(n)\}$. The goal has been defined in terms of the same feature measured at a later time. The underlying concept of a univariate time series is that the forecast of a future value is directly related to prior values. If the population is relatively constant, there are many cases implicit in the series. Given a series $t(1) \ldots t(i) \ldots t(n)$, a window or time lag can be specified for considering related predecessor time points. Consider the series of Figure 3.3, with a window, or time lag, of five time units. This series can be translated into five cases in a standard spreadsheet in Figure 3.4, where the last column is the goal.

Once a time lag or window is specified, transforming a time series into a standard case format becomes a case alignment problem. The cases correspond to the current and previous values at each moment in time. A regression method can use these data to simulate and forecast the next future value. Because the univariate time-series problem is a relatively narrow type of problem, specialized methods have been developed that can explore solutions without any special data preparation. We will consider many more complex and hybrid uses of time series, and these problems can be solved by the generalized prediction methods.

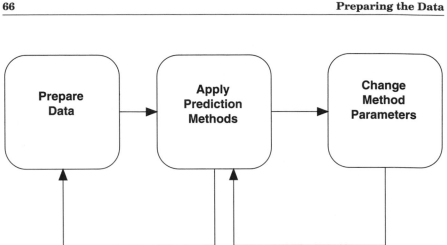

Figure 3.5: Iterative Data Preparation Model

Two issues must be resolved when data preparation proceeds in this style.

- The best time lag must be determined by the usual evaluation techniques for a varying complexity measure using independent test data. Instead of the paradigm of expecting to prepare the data once and turning them over to the prediction programs, additional iterations of data preparation are considered, as illustrated in Figure 3.5.

- While the typical goal is to predict the next unit in time, a period that corresponds to the immediate future, a goal can be any number of units in the future, the lead time. For example, the time units may be months and the objective is to forecast next year's sales for the same time period. The case is $\{\ldots t(n-12), t(n)\}$, where $t(n-12)$ is the current time and $t(n)$ is the forecast for next year. The windows for lag time and lead time need not match. In Chapter 7, an application is examined where a window of two weeks is used to project to the upcoming week. In general, the farther out in the future, the more difficult, and less reliable, the forecast.

3.4.2   Composing Features from Time Series

The spreadsheet representations of features and cases for a time series are relatively close to raw data. In Section 3.5, we will look at many hybrid problems that include univariate time series as a component of a much larger problem. The time units can be relatively small, enlarging the numbers of features to be examined from earlier points in time. A simple time series may become a high-dimensional problem. Thus, we might consider abstracting the time series into higher-level components. Besides the potential for high dimensions, there is often a great difference between the theoretical fit to a time series in ideal laboratory conditions and the real-world experience of application. Time-series analysis is of great interest for marketing and business forecasting, and several comparative studies have been made for prediction methods. While the previous approaches have emphasized linear models, leaving some room for improvement, much can be learned from these practical results, particularly the comparisons on large numbers of forecasts for business-related time series.

In theory, many cases can be extracted from time-series data. In practice, many cases may be historical relics that should not be used to forecast. Using all the cases implies that the population is constant. With times series, this hypothesis may be untenable. For engineering applications, the data are often stable, but even then operating conditions can change or error conditions can be repaired that change the population characteristics. For business and social applications, new trends can develop that make older data less reliable. This leads to a greater emphasis on recent data, possibly discarding the oldest portions of the series. Thus, the sample of cases may have a fixed size n, and only the n most recent cases are used for analysis. Similarly, in describing a case, only the most recent m features may be used, and even then, they may not be given equal weight. These decisions must be given careful attention and are somewhat dependent on knowledge of the application and past experience. When new time-series data are recorded, the analysis should be repeated to determine new trends or possible changes in conclusions.

Let's look at some approaches to extracting and summarizing characteristics of a time series.

3.4.2.1   Current Values

The most recent value is often a good predictor of the value for the immediate next period. Given the current value, $t(i)$, with goal $t(i + 1)$, the feature $t(i)$ is typically very helpful. Many times it is better to specify the goal as a difference, $t(i + 1) - t(i)$. Using a ratio, like $t(i + 1)/t(i)$, to indicate the percentage change is also reasonable. A goal that computes a difference is particularly useful for logic methods, such as decision trees or rules, that have no natural mechanism for deducing differences. Both standard logic and distance regression use a mean or median of target values as their answer. When $t(i + 1)$ is the goal, they cannot adapt to a changing trend that projects a number outside the range already encountered in the sample. Using the difference is preferred for these prediction methods. When the goal is a net change, the current difference, $t(i) - t(i - 1)$, should be a useful feature. In general, the style for the goal should match the feature specifications. When differences or ratios are used to specify a goal, features measuring differences or ratios may also be advantageous. Empirical studies have shown the importance of the current value as a predictor of the next value in a univariate time series. These conclusions have been drawn from the analysis of many business-related time series that are subject to seasonal variations. Seasonal adjustments may be necessary even when the current value is forecast for the next period.

3.4.2.2   Moving Averages

Cases are specified in terms of a goal and a time lag or window of size m. One way of summarizing these m features is to average them. A single average summarizes the most recent m features for each case; and for each increment in time, the oldest point is discarded and the next point is included, hence the name "moving average" as described in Equation 3.4. Knowledge of the application can aid in specifying reasonable sizes for m; error estimation should validate these choices. For some applications, the total count is of interest, not the average. In Equation 3.4, if divisor m is discarded, the feature is simply the total count over a window of size m.

$$ma(i,m) = \frac{1}{m} \sum_{j=i-m+1}^{i} t(j) \qquad (3.4)$$

The moving average weighs all time points equally in the average. Its model of the world is characterized by Equation 3.5, where values are expected to have some random variations. The objective is to smooth neighboring time points by a moving average to reduce the random variation and noise components.

$$t(i) = mean(i) + error \qquad (3.5)$$

Another type of average is an exponential moving average that gives more weight to the most recent time periods. It is described recursively in Equation 3.6, where p is some value between 0 and 1. For example, if p is 0.5, the most recent value, $t(i)$ is equally weighted with the computation for all previous values in the window, where the computation begins with averaging the first two values in the series. As usual, the value of p is determined by application knowledge or empirical validation.

$$ema(i,m) = p * t(i) + (1-p) * ema(i-1, m-1)$$
$$ema(i,1) = t(i) \qquad (3.6)$$

As a single predictor in a business-related time series, the exponential moving average, $ema(i,m)$, has performed very well for many applications, usually producing results superior to the moving average, $ma(i,m)$. The moving average, $ma(i,m)$, measures more of the past, and is somewhat of a midpoint measure of values in the window on time. There is less known about general performance when several of these features are used in a multivariate setting and combined by a prediction program. When used alone as a single predictor, neither type of moving average can spot a new trend, which is discussed next.

3.4.2.3 Trends

Moving averages summarize the recent past, but spotting a change in trend may improve forecasting performance. Even with a changing population, the trend can be helpful in extrapolating to new circumstances.

Characteristics of a trend can be measured by composing features that compare the recent measurements to those of the more distant past. Two simple comparative features are useful:

- $t(i) - ma(i, m)$

- $ma(i, m) - ma(i - k, m)$

The first composite feature is the difference between the current value and a moving average. The second feature measures the difference between two moving averages, usually of the same window size. As usual m, the window size, is determined by prior knowledge or experimentation and testing. In a multivariate setting, several features with different window sizes can be prepared simultaneously and the prediction programs can make decisions about which is best. In Chapter 7, we describe an application where the time units are 30 seconds, and a difference in two moving averages, lagging by five minutes, is used to measure the trend of flow of resources into a plant. For some applications a ratio, such as $t(i)/ma(i, m)$, may be preferable.

3.4.2.4 Seasonal Adjustments

The main components of summarizing features for time series are (a) current values, (b) smoothed values by moving averages and (c) current trends. For some time series, particularly business-related time series, seasonal factors have an important influence on forecasting. There are seasons when the series noticeably changes, and these times or seasons will recur during some periodic, often yearly, cycle. For example, air conditioner sales or housing starts slump during the winter and increase during the summer. Seasonal adjustments to time series are tricky and imperfect. But for many times series, seasonal adjustments are essential for forecasting accuracy. Usually, it is known in advance that seasonal factors strongly influence a given time series. There are methods for decomposing a time series into subcomponents such as a smooth seasonally adjusted curve, a seasonal adjustment constant for each season and a random noise component. One useful analytical forecasting strategy is to seasonally adjust the complete time series $t(i)$, make a forecast using the adjusted data, $t'(i)$, and then remove the seasonal adjustment from the answer.

$$t'(i) = \frac{t(i)}{s(i)} \tag{3.7}$$

$$s(i) = \frac{t(i)}{ma_c(i,m)} \tag{3.8}$$

A technique that has been employed successfully to seasonally adjust time series is Equation 3.7, where $s(i)$ is the seasonal adjustment at time i. Each member of the original time series is divided by a stored constant to produce a new seasonally adjusted time series. The seasonally adjusted series $t'(i)$ is used for training, and $t(i+k)$ is found by forecasting $t'(i+k)$ and then de-adjusting for the season, that is, multiplying the answer by $s(i+k)$, where $s(i+k)$ has been derived from prior seasons. Seasonal adjustments $s(i)$ are computed in Equation 3.8 from a moving average, $ma_v(i,m)$, where window size, m, is the number of seasons in a complete cycle, for example, 52 weeks or 4 quarters in a yearly cycle. Instead of a trailing moving average for $ma_c(i,m)$, where the current $t(i)$ is the last point in the moving average, a centered moving average is used, where $t(i)$ is the midpoint as in Equation 3.9 for a centered moving average of four points.

$$ma_c(i,4) = \frac{t(i) + t(i+1) + t(i-1) + .5 * t(i+2) + .5 * t(i-2)}{4} \tag{3.9}$$

A moving average for a complete year balances out the seasonal influences. Seasonal factors $s(i)$ can be averaged over many years, resulting in a constant adjustment for each season of the year. For example, if the time series represents quarters of the year, then four seasonal adjustment constants are computed. Depending on the quarter of the year, a member of the time series is seasonally adjusted by dividing its value with the corresponding constant for that season. More sophisticated models for seasonal adjustments can be considered for applications with strong seasonal influences. The selection of the appropriate seasonal adjustment should be made by competitive evaluation on test cases.

3.5 Hybrid Time-Dependent Applications

It is quite impressive to see a rich world of representation and analysis for a simple single series of numbers. The transformation of a series into a standard spreadsheet format, with possibly large numbers of features and cases, demonstrates the potential high dimensions that can arise for more complex problem types. Moving beyond a single univariate time series to a variety of complex, time-dependent applications, hybrid representations are needed for assembling and preparing data. In these types of applications, the summarizing features, like moving averages, are essential. We next look at some of these hybrid possibilities, combining characteristics of time series and other standard problem types.

3.5.1 Multivariate Time Series

Analysis of a univariate time series is hardly a knowledge-intensive task. No matter how many ways the data are transformed, knowledge is summarized in a single concept. Even the goal is measured in terms of the same feature. The goal is worthy, but the basis on which forecasts are made often implies a shortage of knowledge about the determining factors of the goal. The immediate extension of a univariate time series is to a multivariate one. Because general prediction methods expect multiple features, the many features abstracted from even single univariate time series can be examined simultaneously.

The concept of a multivariate time series is an extension of the univariate series. Instead of having a single measured value at time i, $t(i)$, multiple measurements $t(i,j)$ are taken at the same time i. For example, multiple measurements are recorded in a commercial plane's black box and are sampled at fixed intervals. These measurements are valuable in finding the cause of an accident. The plane's direction is not solely dependent on just its previous values. It may be a good predictor for the next value of direction, but many other factors are considered by the pilot, like a mountain range directly ahead. In Chapter 7, we consider a control application where multiple measurements for an industrial process are recorded every 30 seconds. Based on these measurements, a change in a control setting may be made. This change cannot be determined solely by examining previous values of the control variable. The rate of consumption of materials and the level of inventory are both critical to the next control setting.

There are no extra steps in data preparation for the multivariate time series. Each series can be transformed into features, and the values of the features at each distinct time, i, are merged into case i. The resultant transformations yield a standard spreadsheet form.

3.5.2 Classification and Time Series

The goal for a times series can readily be changed from regression, predicting the next value in the time series, to classification, which may be more appropriate or easier to solve. The central time-series concept is kept and the data points are recorded at fixed time intervals, but the goal is now true or false, or categorical. For example, multiple measurements can be taken at fixed intervals, such as in a communications network. The goal could be to predict major disasters before they occur, such as the failure of a switch on the network. In Chapter 7, we review a marketing and sales application where the goal is to predict whether sales will rise or fall, not to forecast sales for the upcoming quarter. The simplified goal leads to more effective conclusions for this application. From a data preparation perspective, both classification and regression goals are minor variations of the same standard form.

3.5.3 Standard Cases with Time-Series Attributes

While some data-mining problems are characterized by a single time series, hybrid applications are frequently encountered, having both time series and features that are not dependent on time. The standard case model, having no time-dependency, is the dominant representation. However, each case may have a specific time series that must be transformed into summarizing features. This hybrid application is illustrated in Figure 3.6 where the raw data for the first feature, f_1, consists of a case-specific time series, TS_i. The remaining features, f_k, for each case i, have values $V_{i,k}$ that are already in standard form. The first feature, f_1, is a time series and is not in standard form. It must eventually be mapped into new summarizing features.

In Chapter 7, we describe an application for a major pharmaceutical company that mixes a case-specific time series with a standard case model. The objective of the application is to direct the marketing efforts to those physicians who are most likely to prescribe the company's products. A case is a summary of sales-related information for a specific

Case	f_1	$\cdots$	f_k	G
C_1	$TS_1(t_1),\ldots,TS_1(t_m)$	$\cdots$	$V_{1,k}$	$V_{1,k+1}$
$\cdots$	$\cdots$	$\cdots$	$\cdots$	$\cdots$
C_i	$TS_i(t_1),\ldots,TS_i(t_m)$	$\cdots$	$V_{i,k}$	$V_{i,k+1}$
$\cdots$	$\cdots$	$\cdots$	$\cdots$	$\cdots$
C_n	$TS_n(t_1),\ldots,TS_n(t_m)$	$\cdots$	$V_{n,k}$	$V_{n,k+1}$

Figure 3.6: Hybrid Time Representation

physician. The case includes background information like the physician's specialty and geographic location. Also included in the database of historical information is a time series of the number of prescriptions written by each physician in weekly periods over the last few years.

Hybrid applications are likely to dominate the mix of problems encountered in data-mining applications. These applications are naturally oriented toward cases, and much of the data are already in standard spreadsheet form. The raw time series for each case can be transformed into a set of standard features such as those described in Section 3.4.2.

3.6   Text Mining

A *database* is a depository of diverse types of information. Even if the representation of data is reduced to a spreadsheet model, many different data formats can be accommodated. Free text is the most glaring type of amorphous data that can be readily stored in spreadsheets. Jumping from retrieval of free text to data mining is quite a leap, and might readily be abandoned as too difficult. However, there are effective strategies for preparing text data so that the usual prediction methods are applicable. Once again, the task can be posed as transforming the data into the usual standard spreadsheet format, where all feature values are true or false, or numerical.

Feature extraction from text data fields is a common task for data preparation. In the simplest encounter with text, alphanumeric codes are used to describe measured values. In the most complex variation, free-form text of variable length is stored in a data field. While alphanumeric codes can be readily mapped into unique numerical values, important related problems remain.

- High dimensions: The number of possibilities for alphanumeric codes, which are unordered features, may be very large. In Chapter 7, an application is described where one data field has thousands of possibilities, corresponding to a multitude of replacement parts for home appliances.

- Replication of fields: Multiple instances of the same feature may be described, but the order of the features is not meaningful. For the appliance repair example, a data field denotes the physical part that was replaced. Multiple parts may be replaced to successfully complete a repair. The database design may allocate several data fields for specification of multiple values for the same item. For the example of Chapter 7, the database allocates fields for up to 10 parts that may be replaced on the same service call.

For free text, feature dimensions are potentially unlimited. No longer is there a unique mapping from an alphanumeric code to a true-or-false value. There are too many possibilities of unique words, and many of these possibilities have no predictive use. We next consider the general problem of transforming free text into effective features and measured values. These same techniques may be useful in any environment where high-dimensional data preparation is required, and the raw data are far from standard form.

Text appears to be very far from standard form, suggesting great difficulties in data mining. An analysis of the written word can introduce complicated issues, such as understanding human reading and comprehension. However, some automated text analysis applications have achieved impressive results using relatively simple data preparation schemes. One such application is document indexing, which is usually performed by humans who read documents and assign subjects from a prespecified list of topics. Electronic media organizations generate thousands of documents, each of which must be indexed according to topics. This process allows for effective dissemination and future retrieval.

For a database, the amount of text information corresponding to a case can range from a few words in a data field to complete documents.

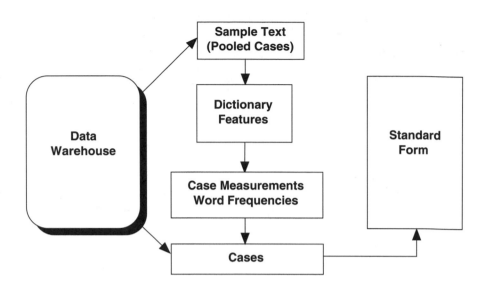

Figure 3.7: Data Preparation for Text Mining

The obvious divergence of text from standard form is the missing specification of the feature set. To map the text data into standard form,
two tasks must be completed: (a) specification of a feature set, and (b)
measured values of these features for each case.

Figure 3.7 gives a general overview of the mapping of text and documents into standard form. The first step is the creation of a word dictionary. This dictionary is the feature set. A word is a set of non-numeric
characters that are preceded and succeeded by word-boundary characters, usually blank or punctuation characters. It's a simple process to
find and sort all words that appear in a collection of text documents.
The documents used to compile a dictionary are assembled in one of two
ways:

- Universal dictionary: all documents

- Local dictionary: documents for a specific topic

Consider the two-class text classification problem, for example, distinguishing between financial and nonfinancial news stories. A local

dictionary uses only the words in the financial stories. If the text fields or documents are for highly specialized topics, a universal dictionary is reasonable. If many wide-ranging topics are covered, with some topics having very low prevalence, then local dictionaries for each topic are indicated. Local dictionaries drastically reduce dimensions, and performance is usually comparable to the universal dictionary.

Of the words found in the document collection, only the most frequently occurring k words are selected. The set of k words contains some words that are of little predictive value, words such as "the" or "it." A separate stopword dictionary is maintained, containing a list of frequently occurring, nonpredictive words. These words are then removed from the main dictionary, and the remaining j frequently occurring words are maintained in the dictionary.

After determining the dictionary, which corresponds to the feature set, the measurements for each case are still missing. In Figure 3.7, the next step is indicated, mapping the text for each case into standard form. This is accomplished by searching for the presence of each dictionary word in the text of each case. If the word is found, the value of the measurement is true; otherwise it is false. Alternatively, a frequency count for each word in the document can be measured for each case. Frequency counts usually give slightly better performance and reduce the complexity of the final solutions. The final result of these transformations is a standard spreadsheet form that can be used by prediction methods.

Whether a database contains complete documents or just simple text fields, the process of mapping text to standard form is the same. These steps are summarized as follows:

- Data: collect and pool text from data fields.

- Preliminary features: find k most frequent words.

- Filter: remove known useless words.

- Extracted features: remaining j words become features.

- Case measurements: check each case for presence or frequency of the j extracted words.

The choice of k, the number of words, depends on experimental testing or constraints on the dimensions of the prediction programs. Experience with local dictionaries in text mining suggests that performance does not increase greatly with dictionaries larger than 200 words, and sometimes as few as 50 words are sufficient for binary classification applications.

3.7   Bibliographic and Historical Remarks

The spreadsheet model of data is the modern version of a matrix of numbers. Data are prepared for one of two types of goals, classification or regression. These are the classical types of statistical prediction. If a prespecified goal is not possible, there are automatic clustering techniques for determining classes, such as the k-means clustering procedure, which is described in Chapter 4.

Data smoothing is implicit in many regression methods, which can be considered global function smoothers. Moving averages are also smoothers, adjusting for randomness and noise. A number of simple data smoothers are discussed in [Tukey, 1977]. Two models of smoothing dominate the literature. The classic concept is the replacement of a range of values with a fixed constant value over local portions of the function. This results in discontinuities of points that appear similar in the original data. The alternative view of smoothing is as a more dynamic process. Data are locally smoothed by moving windows over which the values are averaged, or data can be smoothed by local functions, such as linear functions. These more complicated smoothers are usually not associated with data preparation and are integral to prediction methods. See [Friedman and Stuetzle, 1981] for a discussion of these two schools of thought on smoothing. With big data, the distinction between these models may diminish because more data are available to allow for more local smoothed regions.

Normalizations are usually valuable for case-based methods and some weighted methods. Missing data present difficult problems for all methods, but the logic methods may have the advantage, particularly the decision-rule methods. A comparison of techniques for inducing decision trees with missing data is found in [Quinlan, 1989].

Time-series data represent a classical problem with many specialized statistical models. Informative comparative reviews from the applied perspective are found in [Makridakis et al., 1984; Chatfield, 1988] and [Makridakis et al., 1993]. For applications of business-related time-series data, the simpler techniques have done surprisingly well in forecasting the values of the immediate upcoming period. Examples of new approaches to this classic problem are found in [Masters, 1995] and [Chatfield, 1993]. An example of a complete seasonal-adjustment model is given in [Cleveland and Devlin, 1982]. The univariate time series is hardly a paragon of large-scale data mining, particularly when many of the implied cases become obsolete with time. Large numbers of data-mining applications will have time-dependent data, and previous experience with applied time series is an excellent source of background knowledge [Fildes and Makridakis, 1995].

Research on text analysis has changed character with the revolution in electronic document storage and retrieval. The emphasis has shifted from linguistic understanding of sentence structure to a statistical analysis of word patterns. Research results in text mining demonstrate that a comprehensive statistical analysis of word frequencies in labeled documents combined with prediction techniques can lead to effective text classification systems [Lewis, 1992; Apté, Damerau and Weiss, 1994].

4

Data Reduction

The data have been prepared and presented in the standard spreadsheet form of Table 4.1, and expectations are high for mining the data. Time and energy have been expended in composing the features and transforming the data, and we hope to see some positive results for these efforts. For moderately sized data, the spreadsheet is ready for data mining. For big data, there is an increased likelihood that an intermediate step, *data reduction*, should be tried prior to applying the prediction programs.

In this chapter we take a closer look at data reduction. There are a number of reasons why reduction of big data, shrinking the size of the spreadsheet by eliminating both rows and columns, may be helpful:

- The data may be too big for some prediction programs. In an age when people talk of terabytes of data for a single application, it is easy to exceed the processing capacity of a prediction program.

- The expected time for inducing a solution may be too long. Some programs can take quite a while to train, particularly when a number of variations are considered.

Applying the statistical models of Chapter 2 gives reasonable estimates of future performance from several thousand test cases. Error is estimated after a prediction program finds a solution. The picture is much cloudier for estimating the amount of data needed for training. These data requirements depend on the complexity of the concepts that are implicit in the data. But these concepts are not known prior to

Case	f_1	$\cdots$	f_k	G
C_1	$V_{1,1}$	$\cdots$	$V_{1,k}$	$V_{1,k+1}$
$\cdots$	$\cdots$	$\cdots$	$\cdots$	$\cdots$
C_i	$V_{i,1}$	$\cdots$	$V_{i,k}$	$V_{i,k+1}$
$\cdots$	$\cdots$	$\cdots$	$\cdots$	$\cdots$
C_n	$V_{n,1}$	$\cdots$	$V_{n,k}$	$V_{n,k+1}$

Table 4.1: Standard Spreadsheet Form

data mining; they are the objective of mining. As an extreme example, consider data that are generated from random numbers. There is no predictive value in these data, no matter how large the standard form. No more can be mined from big data than from no data. The extra effort put into mining from all available data is wasted.

Perhaps surprisingly, better answers are sometimes found by using a reduced subset of the available data. Prediction programs can potentially fit their solutions to any size data. The bigger the data, the more exceptions that must be fit. Even with completely random data, many programs will first attempt to fit all the training data. By fitting so many exceptions, some prediction programs are more likely to err on the optimistic side, finding some concept that isn't there.

The main theme for simplifying the data is dimension reduction. Can some of these prepared data be discarded without sacrificing the quality of results? There is one additional requirement for techniques that reduce dimensions. Can the prepared data be reviewed and a subset found more quickly than the prediction program takes to train? Without a marked speedup from the time required for mining the original data, little is gained by dimension reduction. Figure 4.1 illustrates the revised process of data mining with an intermediate step for dimension reduction. Dimension-reduction methods are applied to data in standard form. Prediction methods are then applied to the reduced data.

The data are prepared in the standard spreadsheet form of Table 4.1. In terms of the spreadsheet, a number of deletion or smoothing operations can reduce the dimensions of the data to a subset of the original spreadsheet. The three main dimensions of the spreadsheet are

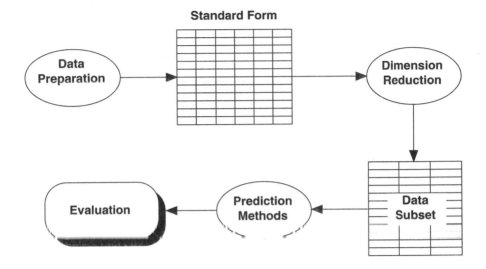

Figure 4.1: The Role of Dimension Reduction in Data Mining

columns, rows and values. Among the operations to the spreadsheet are the following:

- Delete a column (feature)

- Delete a row (case)

- Reduce the number of values in a column (smooth a feature)

These operations attempt to preserve the character of the original data by deleting data that are nonessential or mildly smoothing some features. There are other transformations that reduce dimensions, but the new data are unrecognizable when compared to the original data. Instead of selecting a subset of features from the original set, new blended features are created. The method of principal components, which replaces the features with composite features, will be reviewed. However, the main emphasis is on techniques that are simple to implement and preserve the character of the original data.

Dimension reduction is the goal of the new process that mediates between data preparation and prediction methods. This process can be further decomposed into subprocesses that manipulate either rows or columns of the spreadsheet. Those techniques that delete features could be considered methods for data preparation. Similarly, methods that transform data into a new set of features can also be considered data preparation methods. The subset of data that results from these deletions or transformations maintains the same number of cases. For most applications, the spreadsheet will have many more rows than columns. With big data, the number of cases is likely to grow much more rapidly than the features. Customers and sales may increase, but the number of measurements per customer may not increase much. Thus, deleting a column has a more dramatic effect on data reduction than deleting a row. While not absolutely required, the typical application of these feature-processing methods only occurs once. The original standard form is examined and processed to produce a new spreadsheet that is a subset of the original, but with fewer columns. The processing time to produce the new subset spreadsheet should be relatively quick and can result in a dramatic reduction in feature or value dimensions.

This perspective on dimension reduction is independent of the prediction methods. The reduction methods are general, but their usefulness will vary with the dimensions of the application data and the prediction methods. Some prediction methods are much faster than others. Some have embedded feature selection techniques that are inseparable from the prediction method. The techniques for data reduction are usually quite effective, but in practice are imperfect. Careful attention must be paid to the evaluation of intermediate experimental results so that wise selections can be made from the many alternative approaches.

The first step for dimension reduction is to examine the features and consider their predictive potential. Should some be discarded as being poor predictors or redundant relative to other good predictors? This topic is a classical problem in pattern recognition whose historical roots are in times when computers were slow and most practical problems were considered big problems.

4.1   Selecting the Best Features

The objective of feature selection is to find a subset of features with predictive performance comparable to the full set of features. Given a

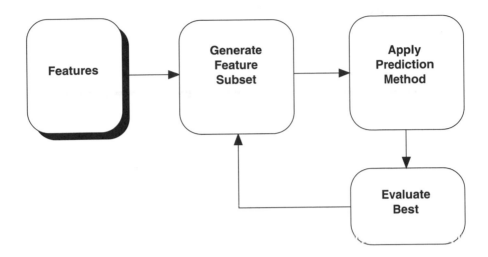

Figure 4.2: Optimal Subset Selection

set of features, m, the number of subsets to be evaluated is finite, and a procedure that finds an optimal solution is described by Figure 4.2. Subsets of the original feature set are enumerated and passed to the prediction program. The results are evaluated and the feature subset with the best result is selected. However, there are obvious difficulties with this approach:

- For large numbers of features, the number of subsets that can be enumerated is unmanageable.

- The standard of evaluation is error. For big data, most prediction methods take substantial amounts of time to find a solution and estimate error.

For practical prediction methods, an optimal search is not feasible for each feature subset and the solution's error. It takes far too long for the method to process the data. Moreover, feature selection should be a fast preprocessing task, invoked only once prior to the application of prediction methods. Simplifications are made to produce acceptable and timely practical results. Among the approximations to the optimal approach that can be made are the following:

- Examine only promising subsets.

- Substitute computationally simple distance measures for the error measures.

- Use only training measures of performance, not test measures.

Promising subsets are usually obtained heuristically. This leaves plenty of room for exploration of competing alternatives. By substituting a relatively simple distance measure for the error, the prediction program can be completely bypassed. In theory, the full feature set includes all information of a subset. In practice, estimates of true error rates for subsets versus supersets can be different and occasionally better for a subset of features. This is a practical limitation of prediction methods and their capabilities to explore a complex solution space. However, training error is almost exclusively used in feature selection.

These simplifications of the optimal feature selection process should not alarm us. Feature selection must be put in perspective. The techniques reduce dimensions and pass the reduced data to the prediction programs. It's nice to describe techniques that are optimal. However, the prediction programs are not without resources. They are usually quite capable of dealing with many extra features, but they cannot make up for features that have been discarded. The practical objective is to remove clearly extraneous features—leaving the spreadsheet reduced to manageable dimensions—not necessarily to select the optimal subset. It's much safer to include more features than necessary, rather than fewer. The result of feature selection should be data having potential for good solutions. The prediction programs are responsible for inducing solutions from the data.

4.2   Feature Selection from Means and Variances

In the classical statistical model, the cases are a sample from some distribution. The data can be used to summarize the key characteristics of the distribution in terms of means and variance. If the true distribution is known, the cases could be dismissed, and these summary measures could be substituted for the cases. Larger numbers of cases would improve estimates of means and variances, but the number of descriptive statistics do not change. Representing data in this way greatly reduces dimensions, with the spreadsheet replaced by means and variances.

The main weakness in this approach is that the distribution is not known. That's really what the prediction program does; it finds the distribution. If it's assumed to be a normal curve, the mathematics can work out very well, but this may in fact be a poor assumption. Instead, without knowing the shape of the curve, the means and variances can be viewed as heuristics that guide the feature selection process.

The goal is to filter the features, not to find a solution to the complete prediction problem. In general, samples of two different classes can be examined, and the means of feature values compared, normalized by the variances. If the means are far apart, interest in a feature increases; it has potential in terms of distinguishing between the two classes. If the means are indistinguishable, interest wanes in that feature. It may be a heuristic, non-optimal approach to feature selection, but it's consistent with practical experience in the triage of features.

There are many variations on the theme of means and variances for feature selection. Let's review the most intuitive methods that should prove effective for most applications.

4.2.1 Independent Features

Given a classification problem, the feature means of the classes can be compared. For two classes, the significance test mentioned in Chapter 2 is an effective yet simple basis of comparison. Equations 4.1 and 4.2 summarize the test, where A and B are the same feature measured for class 1 and class 2, respectively, and n_1 and n_2 are the corresponding numbers of cases.

$$se(A - B) = \sqrt{\frac{var(A)}{n_1} + \frac{var(B)}{n_2}} \qquad (4.1)$$

$$\frac{|mean(A) - mean(B)|}{se(A - B)} > sig \qquad (4.2)$$

The mean of a feature is compared in both classes without worrying about its relationship to other features. With big data and a significance level of two standard errors, it's not asking very much to pass a statistical test indicating that the differences are unlikely to be random variation. If the comparison fails this test, the feature can be deleted. What about the 5% of the time that the test is significant but doesn't show up? These slight differences in means are rarely enough to help in a prediction problem with big data. It could be argued that even a higher significance level is justified in a large feature space. Surprisingly, many features may fail this simple test.

What about comparisons of means for more than two classes? The pairwise comparison is accurate, and we need not try to overplay our hand. For k classes, k pairwise comparisons can be made, comparing each class to its complement. A feature is retained if it is significant for any of the pairwise comparisons. The objective is filtering, and it is better to err on the side of retention rather than deletion.

A comparison of means is a natural fit to classification problems. It is more cumbersome for regression problems, but the same approach can be taken. For the purposes of feature selection, a regression problem can be considered a pseudo-classification problem, where the objective is to separate clusters of values from each other. A simple screen can be performed by grouping the highest 50% of the goal values in one class, and the lower half in the second class.

4.2.2 Distance-Based Optimal Feature Selection

If the features are examined collectively, instead of independently, additional information can be obtained about the characteristics of the features. A method that looks at independent features can delete columns from a spreadsheet because it concludes that the features are not useful. Several features may be useful when considered separately, but they may be redundant in their predictive ability. For example, the same feature could be repeated many times in a spreadsheet. If the repeated features are reviewed independently, they all would be retained even though only one is necessary to maintain the same predictive capability. In practice, the decision is not as stark as this. There are subtle overlapping decision regions in the feature set.

Under assumptions of normality or linearity, it is possible to describe an elegant solution to feature subset selection, where more complex relationships are implicit in the search space and the eventual solution. In many real-world situations the normality assumption will be violated, and the normal model is an ideal model that cannot be considered an exact statistical model for feature subset selection. Normal distributions are the ideal world for using means to select features. However, even without normality, the concept of distance between means, normalized by variance, is very useful for selecting features. The subset analysis is a filter, but one that augments the independent analysis to include checking for redundancy. When looked at in these terms, reasonable and effective feature selection strategies emerge.

A multivariate normal distribution is characterized by two descriptors: M, a vector of the m feature means, and C, an $m \times m$ covariance matrix of the means. Each term in C is a paired relationship of features, summarized in Equation 4.3, where $m(i)$ is the mean of the i-th feature, $v(k,i)$ is the value of feature i for case k and n is the number of cases. The diagonal terms of C, $C_{i,i}$, are simply the variance of each feature, and the nondiagonal terms are correlations between each pair of features.

$$C_{i,j} = \frac{1}{n} \sum_{k=1}^{n} [(v(k,i) - m(i)) * (v(k,j) - m(j))] \qquad (4.3)$$

In addition to the means and variances that are used for independent features, correlations between features are summarized. This provides a basis for detecting redundancies in a set of features. In practice, feature selection methods that use this type of information almost always select a smaller subset of features than the independent feature analysis.

Consider the distance measure of Equation 4.4 for the difference of feature means between two classes. M_1 is the vector of feature means for class 1, and C_1^{-1} is the inverse of the covariance matrix for class 1. This distance measure is a multivariate analog to the independent significance test. The difference in means is computed, normalized by the covariance. The inverse of a matrix is analogous to division. Here the distance measure is squared and sample size is not used because there is no accurate significance test that extrapolates to a sampling distribution for the means. As a heuristic that relies completely on sample data without knowledge of a distribution, D_M is a good measure for filtering features that separate two classes.

$$D_M = (M_1 - M_2)(C_1 + C_2)^{-1}(M_1 - M_2)^T \qquad (4.4)$$

We now have a general measure of distance based on means and covariance. The problem of finding a subset of features can be posed as the search for the best k features measured by D_M. If the features are independent, then all nondiagonal components of the inverse covariance matrix are zero, and the diagonal values of C^{-1} are $1/var(i)$ for feature i. The best set of k independent features are the k features with the largest values of $(m_1(i) - m_2(i))^2/(var_1(i) + var_2(i))$, where $m_1(i)$ is the mean of feature i in class 1, and $var_1(i)$ is its variance. As a feature filter, this is a slight variation from the significance test with the independent features method.

The real objective is to find good features and to eliminate redundancies. The covariance matrices usually will not have zeros for most elements. Given the target of k best features, all subsets of k from m features must be evaluated to find the subset with the largest D_M. With big data having many features, this can be a huge search space. However, the search space can be dramatically reduced by branch-and-bound algorithms capable of finding the optimal k features. The key idea that makes an exhaustive search possible is that D_M is monotonic. The largest distance of D_M is for the full set of features, and for any subset of features F, $D_M\{F\} < D_M\{F, i\}$ where i is a feature not in F.

For a two-class problem, and the number of features, m, ranging into the hundreds, it is quite feasible to find the optimal k features for D_M, where k is about 20. This reduction may still seem reasonable for some methods like neural nets that are computationally very expensive. However, for larger values of k, the optimal search has excessive computational requirements. Heuristic algorithms have a far reduced search space and can come close to the optimal D_M solution. These are considered next.

4.2.3   Heuristic Feature Selection

From a statistical perspective, the complete process of selecting features is heuristic because substitutes are used for the error, or assumptions are made about the distributions. In contrast, from a computational perspective, once a target measure such as D_M is accepted, the solution space may be searched exhaustively, yielding an optimal solution. An exhaustive search is usually not feasible, and there are numerous complicating factors, such as determining the number of k best features,

Figure 4.3: Heuristic Feature Subset Selection

that make heuristic approaches essential. These procedures find locally optimal solutions. No single feature can be added or deleted to improve a fixed measure of distance or significance.

The principal steps of an iterative, heuristic procedure are outlined in Figure 4.3. Two subsets of features are maintained: (a) the set of selected features in the current iteration, and (b) the remaining features. The incremental gain for each feature not in the current subset is computed, and the best single feature is added to the current subset. Following this, all current features are individually evaluated for deletion. Again, only one feature is deleted. When no feature is added or deleted, the procedure halts and the current subset is selected as the locally optimal solution. For each iteration, feature subsets can be compared using the measures described earlier. For instance, comparisons for D_M can be as simple as a minimum incremental percentage gain or loss for the full feature set distance. For D_M, a reasonable condition for halting is when a percentage of the full feature set distance, typically 75% to 90%, is exceeded. Much more commonly used is an approximate statistical F-test to compare covariance matrices for the current subset versus the covariance matrices with a single additional feature. This solves the thorny problem of multiple classes because the F-test can compare all covariance matrices simultaneously. The feature with the greatest significance is added, or the feature with the least significance is deleted. When no single feature passes the significance tests, the procedure terminates with the current subset as its locally optimal solution.

Experience with this class of heuristic search procedures suggests that they are effective in selecting a good subset of features for many prediction programs. These procedures are associated with linear discriminants, but they can be considered general-feature filters. When applied to dozens of features, they are very fast, reinforcing their favorable image. With big data, they have a much greater potential for a marked degradation in performance. The complexity of representing and using feature covariance is on the order of m^2, where m is the number of features. Implementations of these programs can reference many matrices in nonsequential order, and with many features, the matrices may not fit in the computer's data cache. Many iterations of addition and deletion of features may be necessary before a solution is found, and an upper limit, such as $2m$, is placed on the number of iterations. Several hundred features may be manageable, but for very large numbers of features, alternative feature selection methods, such as the decision tree of Section 4.4, may be preferable.

4.3   Principal Components

To reduce feature dimensions, the simplest operation on a spreadsheet is to delete a column. Deletion preserves the original values of the remaining data, which is particularly important for the logic methods that hope to present the most intuitive solutions. Deletion operators are filters; they leave the combinations of features for the prediction methods, which are more closely tied to measuring the real error and are more comprehensive in their search for solutions.

An alternative view is to reduce feature dimensions by merging features, resulting in a new set of fewer columns with new values. One well-known approach is merging by principal components. Until now, class goals, and their means and variances, have been used to filter features. With the merging approach of principal components, class goals are not used. Instead, the features are examined collectively, merged and transformed into a new set of features that hopefully retain the original information content in a reduced form.

The most obvious transformation is linear, and that's the basis of principal components. Given m features, they can be transformed into a single new feature, f', by the simple application of weights, as in Equation 4.5.

$$f' = \sum_{j=1}^{m} (w(j) * f(j)) \tag{4.5}$$

A single set of weights would be a drastic reduction in feature dimensions. Should a single set of weights be adequate? Most likely it will not be adequate, and up to m transformations are generated, where each vector of m weights is called a principal component. The first vector of m weights is expected to be the strongest, and the remaining vectors are ranked according to their expected usefulness in reconstructing the original data. With m transformations, ordered by their potential, the objective of reduced dimensions is met by eliminating the bottom-ranked transformations.

In Equation 4.6, the new spreadsheet, S', is produced by multiplying the original spreadsheet S, by matrix P, in which each column is a principal component, a set of m weights. When case S_i is multiplied by principal component j, the result is the value of the new feature j for newly transformed case S_i'.

$$\mathbf{S'} = \mathbf{SP} \tag{4.6}$$

The weights matrix $\mathbf{P}$, with all components, is an $m \times m$ matrix: m sets of m weights. If $\mathbf{P}$ is the identity matrix, with ones on the diagonal and zeros elsewhere, then the transformed $\mathbf{S}'$ is identical to $\mathbf{S}$. The main expectation is that only the first k components, the principal components, are needed, resulting in a new spreadsheet, $\mathbf{S}'$, having only k columns.

How are the weights of the principal components found? The data are prepared by normalizing all features values in terms of standard errors. This scales all features similarly. The first principal component is the line that fits the data best. "Best" is generally defined as minimum euclidean distance from the line, w, as described in Equation 4.7.

$$D = \sum_{\text{all } i,j} (S(i,j) - w(j) * S(i,j))^2 \tag{4.7}$$

The new feature produced by the best-fitting line is the feature with the greatest variance. Intuitively, a feature with a large variance has excellent chances for separation of classes or groups of case values. Once the first principal component is determined, other principal component features are obtained similarly, with the additional constraint that each new line is uncorrelated with the previously found principal components. Mathematically, this means that the inner product of any two vectors—i.e., the sum of the products of corresponding weights—is zero. The results of this process of fitting lines are P_{all}, the matrix of all principal components, and a rating of each principal component, indicating the variance of each line. The variance ratings decrease in magnitude, and an indicator of coverage of a set of principal components is the percent of cumulative variance for all components covered by a subset of components. Typical selection criteria are 75% to 95% of the total variance. If very few principal components can account for 75% of the total variance, considerable data reduction can be achieved. This criterion sometimes results in too drastic a reduction, and an alternative selection criterion is to select those principal components that account for a higher-than-average variance.

Unlike data reduction by feature selection, processing of new data by principal components requires normalization and a linear transformation. The complexity of computation increases significantly with many features. The main weakness of the method is that it makes an advance commitment to a linear model that maximizes the variance of features. Counterbalancing this commitment to linearity is the rich variety of lines produced, so that an eventual solution need not rely on a single linear combination. Most prediction methods would prefer not to commit to linear transformations prior to seeing the data. Instead, they would rather search for solutions in a manageable feature space. Still, the principal components do reduce the feature dimensions, sometimes quite markedly, and are often effective for weighted prediction methods such as neural nets.

The principal component transformations are less appetizing to the logic methods; they emphasize solutions that explicitly use the original features. These logic methods can be used not only for producing final solutions, but also for selecting features.

4.4   Feature Selection by Decision Trees

Several approaches have been described to filter or transform the features into a reduced number of features. The motivation for separating feature selection from prediction is a great difference in the search space and computational time for these tasks.

The logic methods have a different perspective on feature selection. Feature selection is integral to these methods, and they make no distinction between the two tasks. While there is nothing preventing the deletion of columns prior to learning, the tree method is quite capable of doing its own feature selection. The logic approach to feature selection is dynamic and is coordinated with searching for solutions. Other methods are static in selection because learning is separated from feature selection. A decision tree can be used to select features for other methods, such as neural nets, that take substantially more time to search their solution space. Columns from the spreadsheet are deleted when a feature is not used in the decision-tree solution. The reduced spreadsheet is then passed on to a neural network or other time-consuming prediction method.

Using a decision tree for feature selection is particularly advantageous in large feature spaces. Sometimes called *recursive partitioning*, tree induction is not an iterative process. With large feature spaces, applied algorithms for the tree can be much faster than the mean-based methods of feature selection. In contrast to the other techniques of feature selection, decision-tree induction is directly performed with error measures, not substitutes. The decision-tree method is nonlinear, and it evaluates candidate features in the context of related features that have already been selected.

A simple binary tree is adequate for feature selection. For readers unfamiliar with decision-tree methods, a brief review is given in Section 5.4.1. In the simplest form of feature selection, no fancy techniques for tree induction are used: no pruning, no error estimation on test cases, just the covering tree. The goal is to filter the feature set, so that some columns from the original spreadsheet can be deleted. The main interest is the set of features selected by the tree, not the decision-tree structure or the numerical thresholds. These are the features that are output as the answer of the feature selection process, with the remaining, unused features deleted from the spreadsheet. The tree itself is discarded.

When ties in error occur during tree induction, preference should be given to previously selected features. Ties frequently occur near the bottom of the tree where sample size for a decision is small. A more sophisticated tree algorithm that prunes inessential parts of its solution may perform better. Instead of a tree that covers all cases, the tree is pruned using a significance test to weed out the noisy features that are included to obtain a full cover.

Feature selection is the traditional approach to reducing dimensions. In classical statistical prediction methods, such as linear discriminants, the primary goal of feature selection is a simplification of solutions. Instead of a solution using m weights, a subset may be sufficient to achieve similar performance. Most prediction methods can benefit from this approach to data reduction. Logic methods already integrate feature selection with the search for solutions and have an alternative route to data reduction. In contrast to the other prediction methods, the computational complexity of the logic methods is more directly related to the number of values in the spreadsheet, not the number of features. Next, let's examine techniques for reducing the number of distinct values in the spreadsheet.

4.5   How Many Measured Values?

With big data, most selection techniques that delete features must conclude that those features are completely uninteresting. When this form of major surgery can be performed, the reduction in dimensions is obvious. For some prediction methods, there is a less drastic form of action that can be taken to reduce the dimensions of the features. Within a column, the number of distinct values can be counted, and if this number can be reduced, the logic methods will have a valuable data reduction. In contrast to the other methods that use a variety of arithmetic operations on the data, the logic methods' basic operator is just comparison. Using less-than, greater-than, or equal-to operators, the logic methods will examine all values of a feature and compare error measures. With fewer values, fewer comparisons are made. For methods that use arithmetic

Partition	Case-Value Pairs
P_1	(1,1),(2,5),(3,4),(4,3),(5,5),(6,1),(7,2),(8,3),(9,7),(10,3)
P_2	(1,1),(6,1),(7,2)
P_3	(2,5),(3,4),(4,3),(5,5),(8,3),(9,7),(10,3)

Table 4.2: Partitioning Cases

operators, such as multiplication, the number of values is inconsequential to data reduction and predictive complexity.

The logic methods partition data into smaller groups of cases. They examine the feature values for the cases falling within a partition. These methods do not examine the feature values in random order. They perform the following two general tasks for each feature:

- Sort the values

- Check errors at each unique value

In the standard view of this partitioning problem, these tasks are performed dynamically for cases in the partition. For example, in Table 4.2, there are 10 case-value pairs for feature f_i in partition P_1. The binary-tree program splits P_1 into P_2 and P_3. To examine feature f_i in P_1, 10 values are sorted, and then 3 values are put in P_2, and 7 values in P_3. The tree-induction program, or other logic method, spends a major portion of the time sorting values, blind to the repetition of these values. It then checks the error at each unique value.

Blind sorting cannot take advantage of reduced value dimensions. With moderate data, sorting is not very complex. With big data, the overhead for sorting is markedly increased. The alternative is to sort all feature values and associated cases just once, and store the ordered values. In the example, just P_1 is sorted. P_2 and P_3 are effectively sorted by using the order of P_1 and skipping the values that do not match the cases of new partition P_2 or P_3. This approach eliminates sorting, the major computational task of standard logic methods, but creates two new headaches. For each feature, the values in the spreadsheet must be replaced by pointers to the sorted values in a sorted list maintained for each feature. Also, the tree-program, or other logic method, proceeds through all feature values even when the partition contains few cases. The extra overhead is small because it is necessary only to mark whether the case is in the partition, and not to compute error.

The computational expense of sorting just once is low. If the number of feature values is ensured to be small relative to the number of cases, then the computational complexity for logic methods is usually reduced. With fewer values of a feature, a prediction procedure can make fewer comparisons. In real-world applications, many features already have relatively few distinct values, typically when the values are recorded as integers. Even when the number of values is quite large for a feature, perhaps approaching the number of cases, there are techniques to reduce the maximum number of values for a feature to a relatively small number.

A reduction in feature values is usually not harmful for real-world data-mining applications, and it leads to a major decrease in computational complexity. While empirical evidence for this will be provided in Chapter 6, the computational advantage must be balanced by the time necessary to smooth the data to a maximum number of values per feature. In general, the smoothing time is not large because each feature is smoothed independently of other features, and the data are smoothed and prepared only once. Most importantly, the benefits from smoothing the data by reducing values can accumulate over a series of many experiments with the same smoothed data. Some logic methods are iterative; they process the data and partition more than once before reaching a final solution. Reducing the number of values can greatly reduce the dimensions of the search space for solutions.

4.5.1   Reducing and Smoothing Values

Let's look at a model for relating a reduced value space to the original values. A feature in standard form has a range of values, and these values can be ordered from smallest to largest. Using greater-than and less-than operators, a logic method considers only ranges of consecutive values. This leads naturally to the concept of placing the values in bins. For example, the 10 values for P_1 in Table 4.2 could be placed in three bins like those of Figure 4.4.

$$1, 1, 2, \underbrace{3, 3, 3}, \underbrace{4, 5, 5}, 7$$
$$\underbrace{}_{bin1} \quad \underbrace{}_{bin2} \quad \underbrace{}_{bin3}$$

Figure 4.4: Partitioning into Bins

$$\underbrace{1, 1, 1}_{bin1}, \underbrace{3, 3, 3}_{bin2}, \underbrace{5, 5, 5, 5}_{bin3}$$

Figure 4.5: Smoothing by Bin Medians

$$\underbrace{1, 1, 2}_{bin1}, \underbrace{3, 3, 3}_{bin2}, \underbrace{4, 4, 4, 7}_{bin3}$$

Figure 4.6: Smoothing by Bin Boundaries

All values in a bin will be merged into a single concept, usually either the mean or median of the bin's values. Using the median for Figure 4.4 yields the bins of Figure 4.5. The mean or median is effective for a moderate or large number of bins.

When only a small number of bins are employed, alternatives to the mean or median should be considered. The boundaries of each bin can be candidates for the thresholds that are examined by the logic-based prediction program. In Figure 4.6, all values in a bin are replaced by the closest of the two boundary values.

Using a mean or median value is an application of the classical view of local smoothing of values. All values are expected to be of the form of Equation 4.8, where *noise* is a random error or a random variance from the mean. The objective is to approximate the original values with fewer values. However, it is possible that the smoothed values will perform better than the original values in some real-world applications. This model of value smoothing explains this phenomenon. Methods that try to reduce values by smoothing will typically use somewhere between 25 and 100 bins. These are generally sufficient to approximate and smooth

the original values. With smoothed values, it is not unusual to see training errors move closer to test error rates, particularly at lower solution
complexities like trees with few nodes. Only training data are smoothed.
New or test data remain unsmoothed, maintaining the original values.

$$value(i) = mean(i) + noise(i) \tag{4.8}$$

A feature can potentially assume as many distinct values as the
number of training cases. Using 50 values to approximate and smooth
the sample feature values can drastically reduce dimensions. For many
applications without real-valued features, the number of features having more than 50 values may be quite small. Yet, unless their values are
smoothed, these few features could absorb much of the processing time.

Although a global maximum of 50 to 100 values is usually quite manageable, for big data some logic methods may need a more substantial
reduction in the maximum values to perhaps no more than 5 or 10. Here
the approximation and smoothing perspective is somewhat blurred, and
instead the objective is to find the best thresholds for decisions. In theory, this is a dangerous task because it should be impossible to pick
the best cutoffs outside the context of other features. Still, some useful
decisions can be made about cutoffs independently of other features,
and the results on many applications can be good. If the target is to
pick only a few best thresholds, then the boundary-value representation
is most suitable. In the most extreme interpretation, the boundaries of
the bins are found, and a new feature is created for each bin. When
the value falls in the bin, the feature value is 1, and zero otherwise.
Thus, a numerical variable is replaced by a series of discrete, Boolean
features. The width of each bin is not necessarily of equal value; the
best boundaries are those that separate the goals the best. This type
of "discretization" is somewhat burdensome, requiring new features for
both the original cases, and new or test cases. Alternatively, a simpler
variation may be used, where each of the original values is mapped
into the closest of the two boundaries in the bin. While some logic-
based prediction programs can only process binary features and use
equality operators, most use less-than or greater-than operators, which
can theoretically duplicate the bins and group consecutive bins.

The problem of reducing values has been described as a clustering
problem. Given a fixed number of bins k, the values should be clustered

in the bins according to some reasonable criteria. Let's discuss next how the clustering problem can be solved.

4.5.1.1 Rounding

In everyday life, numbers are approximated by rounding. The very numbers that are presented in the raw data may have already been rounded. Equation 4.9 is the elementary notion of rounding for decimal whole numbers, where ix is the value to be rounded, and k is the number of rightmost decimal places to round. For example, the number 145 is rounded to 150 with $k = 1$, and rounded to 100 with $k = 2$.

$$iy = int(ix/10^k)$$
$$\text{if } (mod(ix, 10^k) \geq (10^k)/2) \text{ then } iy = iy + 1 \qquad (4.9)$$
$$ix = iy \times 10^k$$

Rounding is a natural type of operation for humans; it's also natural for the computer, and it involves very few operations. Binary units should be used, with the 10 replaced by 2 in Equation 4.9—this allows for better-fitting approximations. Slight adjustments are made for negative numbers and decimal fractions. Numbers with decimals are converted to integers prior to rounding by multiplying by a constant corresponding to the maximum number of needed decimal places. After rounding, the number is divided by the same constant. Negative numbers are converted to positive prior to rounding, and the negative sign is reinstated after rounding.

The time for rounding even with big data is relatively small. Figure 4.7 describes the general procedure for rounding the values of features. Given a maximum number of values for any feature, a feature's values are sorted once, so that the number of distinct values can be counted. The order is recorded and no further sorting is necessary. Starting at 1, k is increased until the number of values is reduced to less than the allowable maximum, typically 50 or 100. Occasionally, smaller maximum values are useful. To some degree, the smoothing can be considered a minor complexity variation, where a single complexity parameter is varied and tested to check for best results.

Input: $\{v_i\}$, a set of feature values
        max, the maximum number of distinct values desired
Initialize s := 1

If set v contains fractions, multiply all values with a constant
    so that only integers are obtained

Sort $\{v_i\}$

Repeat
        num := number of unique values in $\{v_i\}$
        If *num* $\leq$ *max* quit repeat loop
        s := s + 1
        For each value in original $\{v_i\}$
                If negative, multiply by -1
                Round using Equation 4.9 with $k = s$, base=2
                Reverse to negative number if necessary
        Next value
Forever

Divide all values by earlier constant to get back fractions
Output the modified set $\{v_i\}$

Figure 4.7: Value Reduction by Rounding

Rounding is an egalitarian approximator that considers the full spectrum of values. It treats all distinct values as equals, cares not about the frequency of distinct values. It is also oblivious to the goal values and doesn't try to be extra smart and compute statistical properties of the distribution. If the maximum number of values is too small, rounding may be susceptible to overcompensation for outliers.

4.5.1.2   K-Means Clustering

The value-reduction problem can be stated as an optimization problem. Given k bins, distribute the values in the bins to minimize the average distance of a value from its bin mean. The mean of a bin's values replaces the values in the bin. The values are assigned in sorted order because the logic-based prediction programs induce tests with less-than or greater-than comparisons. Either the mean or median is used, with

Input: $\{v_i\}$ a set of feature values
$\quad\quad k :=$ number of bins

Sort $\{v_i\}$
$n_u :=$ number of unique values in v
For each Bin_i
$\quad\quad Bin_i :=$ all cases from next n_u/k unique sorted v values
end-for

Compute Err_{new} the current global distance from the bin means
Repeat
$\quad\quad Err_{old} = Err_{new}$
$\quad\quad$ Store current partition information in $OldBin_i$
$\quad\quad$ For each $Case_j$ in Bin_i
$\quad\quad\quad\quad$ 1. If Dist$[Case_j,$ Mean$(Bin_{i-1})] <$ Dist$[Case_j,$ Mean$(Bin_i)]$
$\quad\quad\quad\quad\quad\quad$ Move $Case_j$ to Bin_{i-1}
$\quad\quad\quad\quad$ 2. If Dist$[Case_j,$ Mean$(Bin_{i+1})] <$ Dist$[Case_j,$ Mean$(Bin_i)]$
$\quad\quad\quad\quad\quad\quad$ Move $Case_j$ to Bin_{i+1}
$\quad\quad$ Next $Case_j$
$\quad\quad$ Compute Err_{new}
Until Err_{new} is not less than Err_{old}
Output $OldBin_i$

Figure 4.8: Value Reduction by k-Means Clustering

distance usually measured as squared distance for means, and absolute distance for medians.

A variant of k-means clustering can produce near-optimum solutions to this problem. Values are clustered such that no value can be moved to an adjacent bin to reduce the global mean distance. Figure 4.8 describes a procedure for assigning the values $\{v_i\}$ to k bins. The procedure does the following: (a) sorts the values; (b) assigns approximately equal numbers of unique and adjacent sorted v_i to each bin; and (c) moves a v_i to an adjacent bin when that reduces the global distance Err from each v_i to the mean of its assigned bin.

K-means clustering can do a good job of approximating and smoothing the original values. Like rounding, a typical application will be for a maximum of 50 to 100 values. Both rounding and k-means concentrate on approximation. They do not look at the case goals, and do not directly

$$C1 \quad C2$$
$$\overbrace{1\,2} \quad \overbrace{3\,5}$$
$$Bin1 \quad Bin2$$

Figure 4.9: Binning by Class Information

guess the best cutoffs. Next, let's consider techniques that think they can do a good job with even fewer values by looking at class labels.

4.5.1.3 Class Entropy

For a two-class problem, an example of an ideal situation is described in Figure 4.9. Values less than 3 are all in class $C1$, and the remaining values are all in class $C2$. Clearly, looking at class labels has reduced the number of useful values. In general, perfect separation is not possible for the values of a single feature, but there may be ranges of values where overlap is relatively small. This has led to procedures that assign the values to bins in order to minimize the average overlap among classes. The values are lined up in a row with their class labels, and a procedure looks for intervals where classes are relatively pure. Because the features are examined independently, there is a risk that many ranges where class overlap is great may have far less overlap once the cases have been partitioned by other features. Still, the intervals with less overlap are prime candidates for interesting feature thresholds, and if enough bins are allowed, there is a reasonable approximation to the original values.

Class overlap can be measured by entropy as described in Equation 4.10, where the entropy of bin k is measured in terms of the probability of class C_i in the bin. The probability of C_i is the count of class C_i in bin k, divided by the number of values in bin k.

$$ent(k) = \sum_i [-Pr(C_i) * log(Pr(C_i))] \qquad (4.10)$$

Similar to the k-means procedure, a locally optimal procedure can be described for assigning values to bins. The global measure of overlap to be minimized is the weighted average of the bins' entropy as described

```
Input: {vᵢ} a set of feature values
       k := number of bins

Sort {vᵢ}
nᵤ := number of unique values in v
For each Binᵢ
     Binᵢ := all cases from next nᵤ/k unique sorted v values
end-for

Compute Errₙₑw
Repeat
       Errₒₗd = Errₙₑw
       Store current partition information in OldBinᵢ
       For each Binⱼ, j < k
              1. MergedBin := Merge [Binⱼ, Binⱼ₊₁]
              2. Split MergedBin into Bin₁ and Bin₂ such that
                        Err(Bin₁, Bin₂) is minimum
              3. Binⱼ = Bin₁ ; Binⱼ₊₁ = Bin₂
              Next Binⱼ
              Compute Errₙₑw
Until Errₙₑw is not less than Errₒₗd
Output OldBinᵢ
```

Figure 4.10: Value Reduction by Class-Entropy Clustering

in Equation 4.11, where $n(k)$ is the number of values in bin k, and N is the total number of cases.

$$Err = \sum_k [ent(k) * \frac{n(k)}{N}] \qquad (4.11)$$

Figure 4.10 describes a procedure for assigning the values $\{v_i\}$ to k bins. The procedure does the following: (a) sorts the values; (b) assigns approximately equal numbers of unique and adjacent sorted v_i to each bin; (c) temporarily merges the values of two adjacent bins and finds the minimum entropy split of these values into two bins; and (d) cycles through all adjacent paired bins until no change occurs for all bins. Although the procedure is described for classification, the same procedure can be applied to regression where entropy is replaced by the squared or absolute error.

Methods that reduce values by class entropy try to find boundaries that minimize error. With many bins—for example, more than 20—the method can also be considered an approximator, and the mean or median used for the summarizing values in a bin. Feature values could readily number in the tens of thousands, so a reduction by class entropy may be major.

Incremental techniques can be used to find the best set of intervals for a feature's values. A binary tree is induced for each ordered, numerical feature, using only the values of that single feature. The terminal nodes of these trees will be mutually exclusive intervals that are ranges of values for a single feature. During tree induction, nodes are not split when the indicated gain fails to exceed a minimum threshold. The decision to continue splitting can be made by statistical significance testing or information-theory measures of minimum descriptive length. With big data, these techniques will greatly lower the threshold for acceptance of new values, often resulting in many more intervals.

Decision trees use the same entropy measure that has been described for bin optimization. Instead of inducing decision trees, the bin model can readily be modified to produce an incremental solution for the boundary values. Starting with two bins, an entropy solution is found. The number of bins is increased by one, and the process is repeated until the incremental gain in entropy falls below a fixed threshold, such as 1%. The threshold is usually decreased for larger numbers of cases. This solution is quite comparable to that of the decision tree, and usually takes relatively little time. The feature values are sorted only once. The resulting intervals can be used directly as new discrete features, or the nearest boundaries of the interval can replace the feature values. The former necessitates transforming new or test data, while the latter needs no further processing of new or test data.

4.6 How Many Cases?

The largest dimension in the spreadsheet is the number of rows, corresponding to the number of cases. Reducing the number of features or the number of values is a relatively efficient process, bypassing the prediction methods. Deleting a row in a spreadsheet is intimately tied to a prediction method. Case reduction is the most complex form of data reduction because the computationally expensive prediction methods must be invoked more often to determine the effectiveness of case reduction.

In an age when storing terabytes of data is common, the importance of case reduction increases. Are all cases residing in a database needed for effective mining? The efficacy of larger training samples is application dependent, and the appropriate sample size depends on the complexity of the concepts that can be extracted from the data. If the data are all random noise, then no useful concept can be extracted from the data, no matter how large. Other than increasing confidence in a conclusion, additional cases add little when the concept is noise. Similarly, when the concept is relatively simple, the results are unlikely to change even with additional cases, for example, where $X > t$ completely separates two classes. On the other hand, for some applications, results continue to improve with additional cases. Here, the concepts may be more complex, and the large volumes of data can supply more evidence for the correctness of the induced concepts.

A sample may appear to be large in terms of numbers of cases, but may not be large relative to the implicit concepts. Some types of problems tend to require more data than others. Among such problems are the following:

- Multiclass classification: For multiclass classification, at least one concept is usually needed for each class. The more classes, the greater the number of underlying concepts, and therefore, the more cases needed to find them.

- Regression: Regression solutions are often more complex than simple two-class classification solutions. Regression can sometimes be related to multiclassification, where the number of classes is extremely large.

- Low-prevalence classification: Many data-mining applications are very low-prevalence classification. Almost all cases are allotted to the larger class, and far fewer cases for the smaller, usually more interesting class. The same number of cases may not loom as large relative to the potential complexities of describing the smaller class.

Is training with all the cases better than using a random subset? The added data should provide more information for mining concepts from the data, and in theory, the prediction programs should do no worse. In practice, the results of training on all cases should be near the best when compared with variably sized, random subsets of the same data. They need not always be better, and can be slightly worse due to the much larger space of solutions that are examined, some of which may look more promising but fail to hold on new cases.

Increasing the number of cases tends to increase the complexity of induced solutions. With large numbers of cases, error estimates can improve marginally, accompanied by large increases in solution complexity. For example, consider a decision-tree method that can readily cover all cases. The tree induced for all sample data is larger than one induced for a subset of the cases. The tree-induction method, like other methods, must cover more exceptions that are found in the larger sample. The trees can be pruned by such techniques as significance testing, minimum descriptive length, or cases per node, but these measures often increase the tree size as the number of cases grows.

Complexity is readily measured in the terms used to describe solutions. Increased complexity is not desirable, but may be the price to pay for better predictive performance. If the application is related to investment, perhaps minimizing error is primary. If the managers of a business are trying to understand the factors influencing sales, then both error and complexity are important. Increased complexity decreases the interpretability of the solution. Less complex solutions tend to vary less in performance on new samples, which is of greatest value when the population may vary over time. When a more complex solution has a much smaller error, usually the complex decision is preferred. However, when two solutions are competitive, the lesser complexity solution may be preferred.

Although near-best answers are typically achieved with the full training sample, a number of reasons have been cited to investigate trends in error and complexity for subsets of the full set of cases. The usual rationale for reducing case dimensions may be of paramount importance: the number of cases may be too many to process in an acceptable time frame. Even when feasibility is assured, obtaining a quick snapshot of potential performance is usually preferred to waiting for answers on all training cases.

The principal approach to case reduction is random sampling. Instead of mining the full collection of cases, random subsamples are collected. Two basic forms of random sampling are effective for case reduction and mining:

- Incremental samples

- Average samples

Mining incrementally larger random subsets of the case data helps spot trends in error and complexity. When the single best solution can only be obtained from the complete collection of cases in the database, the sampling may actually increase the effort to produce a single solution. Even then, the benefits of having a quick overview of potential performance can make the exercise worthwhile. With many real-world applications, experience has shown that performance may level off rapidly after some percentage of the available cases has been examined.

Performance may continue to improve with larger samples of cases, but the capacity of a prediction program may be exceeded. When the results of solutions found from many random samples of size N cases are averaged or voted, the combined solution can do as well or even better than the single solution found on the full collection of cases.

Understanding the expected relationships and trends among error, complexity, and multiple random samples is the key to effective data reduction along the case dimension. Let's consider the static analysis of a single sample before examining the expected trends for many random samples.

4.6.1 A Single Sample

For a single fixed-size sample, many solutions of varying complexity can be generated. These solutions can range from a perfect fit with no error to the default solution of the largest class for classification or the mean value for regression. From a training perspective, the objective is to find the best-fitting solution, the one with minimum true error. A small training error for a complex solution may be optimistic, fitting the training sample but not new cases. The simpler solutions may perform

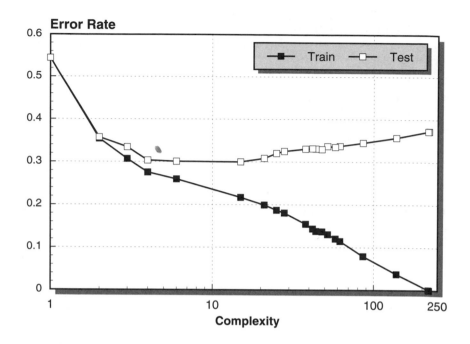

Figure 4.11: A Typical Error and Complexity Relationship

similarly on new cases, but may have a pessimistic bias that does not capture all concepts implicit in a sample. Figure 4.11 illustrates the classic relationship between the apparent training error and the true test error for different complexity solutions extracted from a single sample. Initially with low complexity, both train and test error sharply decrease. As complexity increases, the train error continues to decrease, but the test error flattens. While the objective is the minimum-error and best-fitting solution, in practice some compromise may be made in generating and selecting a solution. No compromise is made in evaluating error. Test error, not train error, must be used to evaluate the adequacy of a sample and its cases.

If the complexity of a solution is fixed, projections of future performance can be made from the train and test errors. As the number of cases increases, eventually the train and test errors approach the same values. With large numbers of cases, it is quite common to see trees of small size or neural nets with few hidden units have the same train and test error. For greater-complexity solutions, the train error is more optimistic than the test error. With enough data, these two estimates converge. The number of cases necessary to guarantee convergence of the two estimates can be huge for most higher-complexity solutions. However, when there is a modest number of cases per complexity unit— for example, an average of five cases per terminal tree node or weight— then a rough estimate of future performance can be made. For a solution of fixed complexity, future performance with much larger numbers of cases is roughly the average of the train and test error. Do not expect the error of a solution of fixed complexity to continue to decrease with unlimited new cases. There are rough indications in a single sample of where the limit is. To improve performance beyond that limit, complexity must be increased.

4.6.2   Incremental Samples

A principal approach to case reduction is to train on increasingly larger random subsets of cases, observe the trends and stop when no progress is made. The subsets should take big bites from the data, so that the expectation of improving performance with more data is reasonable. A typical pattern of incremental subsets might be 10%, 20%, 33%, 50%, 67% and 100%. These percentages are reasonable, but can be adjusted based on knowledge of the application and the number of available cases. The smallest subset should be substantial, typically no fewer than 1,000 cases. For low-prevalence situations, many more cases may be needed in the smallest subset. Initial percentages should be chosen to provide a quick snapshot of performance, and can be increased gradually to the full sample of cases. Because a series of experiments may be needed, most other types of decisions are best made prior to the incremental random sampling. This includes tuning the various program parameters and feature or value reduction, tasks that usually can be performed relatively rapidly, and may not need all available cases when the sample is very large. A smaller subsample need not be a complete subset of a new larger, random subsample.

For a single sample, error is plotted relative to complexity. Eventually, a solution is selected, usually close to the minimum error. Error

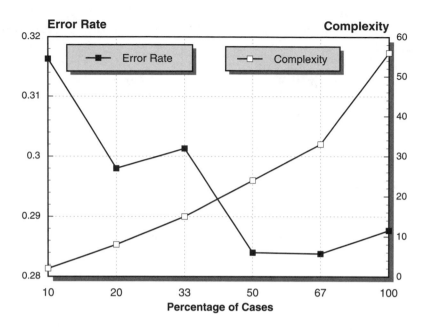

Figure 4.12: A Sample Trend for Error and Complexity

and complexity can be plotted relative to increasing sample size. Figure 4.12 is an example of such a graph for an application in Chapter 6. The central theme is to observe the trend and net change in error and complexity. As illustrated in Figure 4.13, a decision is made prior to the next increment of random sampling whether further experimentation is warranted. The decision could be to abandon further testing, or to jump to a much larger sample, which is computed as a low-priority task with little hope of better results.

The general expectation is that substantial amounts of new data should lead to better performance, and that the complexity of the solution should be acceptable. Before moving to a larger subset, the net changes in error and complexity are examined. Is the error smaller? Is complexity increasing much more than error is decreasing? If solution interpretability is important, is the current complexity acceptable? If error is not decreasing much, is the increased complexity worth it,

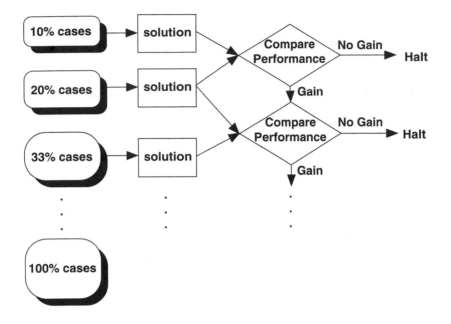

Figure 4.13: Incremental Sampling and Mining

particularly when the population may change in the future? These are judgments that are made in the heat of battle, with full knowledge of the application. However, when solution performance does not improve for a very substantial increment in random sample size, the prospects are not good for a future, large increase in performance.

4.6.3 Average Samples

A data warehouse may contain huge numbers of cases—too many for prediction program L, which has a maximum capacity of N cases. All is not lost. Data are mined not from a single random sample of N cases, but from k random samples of N cases. Instead of finding a solution for the single sample of all cases in the warehouse, solutions from different samples can be averaged as described in Figure 4.14. The same prediction method is applied to many different samples of the same size, producing a solution for each sample. When a new case is presented,

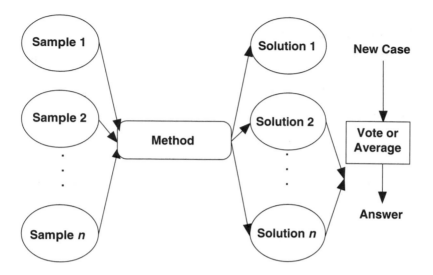

Figure 4.14: Combining Solutions from Different Samples

an answer is given by each solution. The final answer is reached by averaging the answers for regression, or by plurality-wins voting for classification.

Case reduction is achieved by presenting only N cases to prediction method L, far fewer cases than the full set in the data warehouse. However, instead of training on a single sample and finding one solution, k samples are obtained and k solutions are found.

How does the performance of the averaged solution compare to the single solution found on all cases in the warehouse? The answer may come as a surprise. Averaged or voted solutions usually have less error than single solutions. If sufficient samples are taken, the average of their solutions can produce the same result as much larger samples. In Chapter 2, mean error was described in terms of three components: the error of the best solution, bias and variance. Averaging or voting solutions may eliminate most of the error due to variance. If answers averaged or voted from many samples are the same as the answers for pooling those samples, then no additional bias is introduced with smaller samples. Experience shows that averaged solutions for small samples can be as effective as those for larger samples, particularly when the sampling techniques described in Section 5.7.2 are used.

Averaging solutions over many samples is an important technique for case reduction. Its potential for minimizing error is also highly significant. If the error due to variance is eliminated, and no bias is introduced into the solutions, then the averaged solutions can approach the performance of the best solution.

4.6.4   Specialized Case-Reduction Techniques

For some specialized types of problems, alternative techniques can be helpful in reducing the number of cases. These case-reduction techniques are not universally applicable or effective, but sometimes they can dramatically reduce the number of cases and yield good results. The theme of these techniques is that a single, key characteristic of the cases can be used to eliminate some of the cases.

4.6.4.1   Sequential Sampling over Time

For time-dependent data, the number of cases is determined by the frequency of sampling. The sampling period is specified based on knowledge of the application. If the sampling period is too short, most cases are repetitive and few changes occur from case to case. This weakens the prospects for data mining for two reasons:

- The number of cases is too large.

- The prevalence of uninteresting cases is too high.

For time-series data, the windows for sampling and measuring features should be optimized. Often this requires additional experimentation. Case dimensions shrink in proportion to an increase in the sample period. For some applications, increasing the sample period causes no harm, and can even be beneficial when the original time period is too short.

4.6.4.2   Strategic Sampling of Key Events

The sampling interval is a global characteristic of time that affects all cases equally. Another view of the cases is to consider some characteristic that might be used to separate the cases into interesting cases and those that can be put aside. The interesting cases are analyzed in detail, and the others are all assumed to be noise.

An example of this type of case reduction occurs in regression problems where the net change of a measurement is the goal. Cases might be filtered by discarding all cases having a net change below a fixed threshold of absolute net change. In Chapter 7, a control problem is described, where all changes in instrument settings are recorded. Data are sampled every 30 seconds, and hundreds of thousands of cases are assembled. However, knowledge of the application leads to the deletion of all cases where the net change is small because these deleted cases are random noise, equivalent to no change in the control settings. The remaining cases represent critical changes in the controls, and are used as input data to prediction methods that find very effective solutions.

Besides drastically reducing the number of cases, focusing on known critical events modifies the implied prevalence of events. In the control application, the number of critical changes is small relative to the number of available cases. Most available cases are discarded. If a prediction program were applied to data including the discarded cases, the critical cases would be overwhelmed, leading to poor solutions. Although the prevalence of events is greatly modified, the results are positive.

4.6.4.3   Adjusting Prevalence

Instead of a global characteristic like window size or magnitude of change, the prevalence of cases might be directly adjusted. Given a low-prevalence class, prevalence is increased by repeating (or weighting) cases in the training sample. This has a similar effect to increasing the cost of error for a class. Repeating cases increases the sample size. An alternative for boosting prevalence is to keep the low-prevalence cases intact, while including a random subset of a larger class in the training sample, perhaps a balanced 50% prevalence of each for binary classification. However, without prior knowledge of the application, this is an optimist's outlook, and it usually leads to disappointment in the real world. On occasion, a doubling of the prevalence of the training data for a small class may actually produce better results on unfiltered new data. The increased prevalence will goad the prediction programs to extract more complex and seemingly better performance from the data. In general, though, when a large adjustment is made in the true prevalence, the solution must be adjusted to reflect the true prevalence. A solution, which performs with 90% accuracy for a doubled prevalence, may actually have double the originally estimated error when new cases are presented. This phenomenon can be detected by training with increased prevalence, but getting test estimates with test data having the expected prevalence. When a smaller class is known to be more important than the larger classes, the number of training cases may be balanced equally among the classes, effectively increasing the cost of error for the smaller class.

4.7 Bibliographic and Historical Remarks

The traditional approach to reducing dimensions is feature selection. The use of means and variance is the standard statistical representation. Most techniques are heuristic, and a good summary of representative heuristic methods is found in [James, 1985]. The optimal subset algorithm is from [Narenda and Fukunaga, 1977], and the coded branch-and bound-algorithm is given in [Ridout, 1988]. The technique of principal components has had many successful applications in conjunction with pattern recognition or neural net methods. A concise description of the method, also known as the *Karhunen-Loeve expansion*, is found in [Murtagh and Heck, 1987]. Using trees as feature selection filters for other prediction programs has not received wide attention. With big data and very large feature dimensions, tree methods (described in Chapter 5) for feature selection may become the methods of choice for quick feature selection. The preponderance of sorting in the computation of algorithms for decision-tree induction was demonstrated in [Catlett, 1991]. Without big data, the sorting factor is of little consequence. The efficiencies of presorting of values for decision-tree induction has been described in [Mehta, Agrawal and Rissanen, 1996]. In more computationally intensive logic approaches, such as [Weiss and Indurkhya, 1993], value reduction has been added to pre-resorting the values. The general technique of k-means clustering is given in [Hartigan and Wong, 1979]. The use of decision trees and class entropies to discretize features into a few intervals has been studied in [Catlett, 1991; Fayyad and Irani, 1993; Dougherty, Kohavi and Sahami, 1995]. For nearest-neighbor methods, some attention has been given to case reduction and editing [Hart, 1967] after the predictions for the complete set of cases are known. The classic relationship between train and test error for a single sample is described in [Breiman, Friedman, Olshen and Stone, 1984]. The expected convergence of train and test errors, for a fixed complexity solution with increasing numbers of cases, is described in [Cortes, Jackel, Solla, Vapnik and Denker, 1994].

Before the advent of very fast workstations, it was quite common in the machine learning literature to report results in an incremental fashion for a single application, demonstrating how well the methods scaled with increasing data. With moderately sized datasets and fast prediction methods, interest shifted to accurate error estimation on a broad set of real-world applications. In an era of big data, incremental comparisons return to prominence. The great potential for case reduction and reduced error of averaged solutions taken from random samples of big data is described in [Breiman, 1996a; Breiman, 1996b; Breiman, 1996c].

5

Looking for Solutions

5.1 Overview

Once the data are prepared, the search for solutions begins. Many prediction methods are available and accessible; most can readily be applied to data described in standard form. Readers may be familiar with existing methods and already have their favorites. After all, the study of these methods has been the principal subject of research on data analysis. Here, we give a quick overview of some of the strongest and most widely used prediction methods. The objective is not to review the methods in a comprehensive mathematical manner, a subject that is covered in many other books. Instead, our focus is on the types of solutions provided by the methods and their relationship to the data. How is a solution represented? How is it applied to new data? What special data preparation issues affect the search for a good solution using the method? What are the effects of high-dimensional data on the method? What is the right-size solution, and how does it explain its reasoning? In a break with tradition, this review of prediction methods does not give details of the actual prediction algorithms. The methods are available as prepackaged programs. Instead, we'll look at the many other important issues that affect a method for mining big data.

The prediction methods are grouped according to three types of solutions: (a) math, (b) distance or (c) logic. The math and logic solutions describe solutions as direct operations on the measurements of a new case. Distance solutions obtain answers for a new case by measuring similarity to other stored cases. Representative prediction methods are reviewed for each of the three types of solutions, and a standard set of questions are posed and answered for each prediction method. These methods are later applied to the real-world data-mining applications to be described in upcoming chapters. All but one of these applications are classification, but many regression methods are also effective for classification.

5.2   Math Solutions

Math solutions combine the feature values using mathematical operators such as addition and multiplication. The solutions of alternative methods differ in their representations and their valid mathematical operations. Three types of math solutions for data mining are reviewed: (a) linear, (b) neural networks and (c) nonlinear statistical solutions.

5.2.1   Linear Scoring

The classical statistical methods are the linear discriminant and the linear solution of least-squares regression. A simple score is obtained by taking a weighted linear combination of the features. The weighted score is used as an answer in regression or a ranking for classification. When observed on a normalized scale, the more important features usually have weights of greater magnitude that contribute more to the final score.

I. Solution Representation

For regression, a solution is expressed as a single weighted sum of features. In Equation 5.1, the feature values, f_i, are multiplied by weights, w_i, and the answer y is the sum of these products and a constant weight w_0.

$$y = w_1 f_1 + w_2 f_2 + \cdots + w_m f_m + w_0 \qquad (5.1)$$

For classification, a separate linear score is found for each class. For m features and c classes, the linear discriminant solution is a set of c

$$23.544f_1 + 23.588f_2 + (-16.431)f_3 + (-17.398)f_4 + (-86.308) = d_1$$
$$15.698f_1 + 7.073f_2 + 5.211f_3 + 6.434f_4 + (-72.853) = d_2$$
$$12.446f_1 + 3.685f_2 + 12.767f_3 + 21.079f_4 + (-104.368) = d_3$$

Figure 5.1: A Linear Discriminant Solution

equations, each of which is a weighted combination of the m features shown in Equation 5.2.

$$w_{11}f_1 + w_{12}f_2 + \cdots + w_{1m}f_m + w_1 = d_1$$
$$w_{21}f_1 + w_{22}f_2 + \cdots + w_{2m}f_m + w_2 = d_2$$
$$\vdots \qquad (5.2)$$
$$w_{c1}f_1 + w_{c2}f_2 + \cdots + w_{cm}f_m + w_c = d_c$$

Figure 5.1 illustrates a linear discriminant solution for the classical iris data. These data have four features and three classes. A case is classified by replacing the features with measured values in the equations and computing the scores, d_i's. The class with the largest score is selected.

II. Data Preparation and Learning

Classical methods can readily process data that are in standard spreadsheet form. The linear methods, as well as other math methods, are susceptible to two potential problems:

- Categorical features: The classical linear methods expect continuous features. With big data, the conversion of categorical features to multiple binary features is sufficient to mimic continuous features without invoking specialized techniques.

- Missing Values: The math methods have obvious difficulties with missing values. Some of the dimension-reduction techniques can be helpful in dealing with large numbers of missing values.

Classical statistical methods readily obtain the weights for linear solutions. Many efficient implementations are available in statistical packages.

III. Dimension Reduction

The main approach to data reduction for linear methods is feature selection. While the efficiency of inducing linear solutions is high for large numbers of features, a high-dimensional feature space can lead to poor results with large variations in weight magnitudes and potential singularities in matrix inversion routines. Feature selection can be effective in eliminating these difficulties and computing reasonable solutions. Case reduction can help obtain the answer more quickly, but the best linear solutions are usually found from the full sample of cases.

IV. Solution Complexity

Because the solution is always linear, the dimensions of the solution are fixed by the number of features. Some reduction in complexity is achieved by reducing the number of features through feature selection. Occasionally for unnormalized data, a meaningful math solution cannot be found using all features. Difficulties of this type are indicators for feature selection. Feature selection reduces complexity, but rarely produces better results than the full feature set, when a full-set solution is computable. Unlike other prediction methods, increasing complexity is restricted by the linear model.

V. Overall Assessment

Timing. Applying the solution for a particular case is a trivial computation. The induction process is also very fast compared to other prediction methods. The main computational cost is for the inverse covariance matrix, taking $O(m^2)$ time, where m is the number of features. Feature selection using covariance also increases substantially with the number of features. Overall, the classical linear methods are fast.

Explanatory Capabilities. As long as solutions are mapped to two or three dimensions, effective visual presentations can be made for linear solutions. For classification, the metaphor is separation of surfaces representing clusters of cases. For regression, a line through a series of points is an intuitive visual summary of those points. In higher dimensions, visualization is less effective. While visualization is surely a strength of linear solutions, the relative explanatory capabilities of all prediction methods can be considered by directly examining solutions. The linear methods compute a score, and a weight indicates the positive or negative contribution of the feature to the score. Because the solution is limited to a simple form of addition and multiplication of weights with unnormalized data, the method maintains good explanatory capabilities, especially when a few select features have large weights.

Finding a Good Solution. The classical linear methods have performed well on many applications. Solution complexity is restricted to a simple additive score, and for modest case and feature dimensions, a linear model is a good match for data that are unlikely to support greater complexity solutions. For big data, the classical expectations are less likely to hold. Linear solutions may often prove competitive for some data-mining applications. However, experience has shown that occasionally other methods will handily exceed the performance of a linear solution when the data are available to support a higher-complexity solution.

5.2.2   Nonlinear Scoring: Neural Nets

The linear model is a very appealing math solution. It's no wonder that so much research time has been devoted to developing methods that find linear solutions. The most intuitive math is used for scoring, adding weight for positive features and subtracting for negative features. Because linear solutions are easy to obtain, they are good baselines for further investigation. Big data and fast processing make nonlinear math solutions feasible and even imperative, because of their potential for superior performance.

For nonlinear solutions, the universe of math operations is unlimited and complex. Fortunately, a family of nonlinear solutions, called *neural*

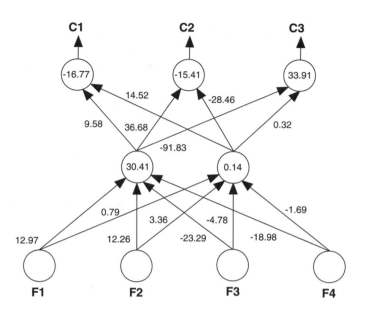

Figure 5.2: A Fully Connected Feed-Forward Neural Network

nets, provide an elegant and powerful approach to prediction. In theory, neural nets are capable of approximating even the most complex functions, yet their math is only slightly more complicated than linear. The nets are capable of producing many solutions; the simplest one is a linear solution.

I. Solution Representation

Neural nets solve regression problems and are readily adapted to classification. The most widely used neural networks are fully connected and feed forward with a single hidden layer. An example of a solution to the iris data is shown in Figure 5.2 with four features, called *inputs,* two intermediate outputs, called *hidden units,* and three final output units, one for each of the three classes. Figure 5.2 illustrates the organization of the network into three layers: input, hidden and output layers. Every node in a layer is fully connected to every node in the layer above it. In addition to weights associated with a link between nodes, each output node adds a constant weight. The computation feeds forward from inputs to outputs without loops. Starting with the linear solution of zero hidden units, a net can have a variable number of hidden units, and these determine the complexity of the classifier.

$$net_j = \sum_{i=1}^{N} W_{ij} I_i + \theta_j \qquad (5.3)$$

$$O_j = \frac{1}{1 + e^{-net_j}} \qquad (5.4)$$

The inputs are the feature values of a case, and these values are combined in Equations 5.3 and 5.4 to compute the outputs. The class with the highest score is selected. Computations are local to each output and involve only connections from the previous layer. The outputs of the first layer are the input values of a case. The hidden outputs compute using the links from the original features, but the final outputs use links from the intermediate hidden nodes. Equations 5.3 and 5.4 show a two-part computation. For each node, j, let there be N input nodes, numbered from $i = 1$ to N. W_{ij} is the weight of the link between i and j, I_i is the input from node i and θ_j is the constant value associated with j. The output of j is computed as shown in Equation 5.4. In the first stage, the computation is strictly linear. If this were the only computation, then the collection of many linear computations remains a linear solution. In the second part of the equation, a simple threshold function is introduced that keeps the range of values at any node between zero and one. This extra "sigmoid" function gives the net its nonlinear powers of approximation.

II. Data Preparation and Learning

The values of the original data should be normalized to numbers having an absolute value of no more than one. Experience has shown that normalized numbers, scaled similarly to the output values, lead to better training. The normalization procedures outlined in Chapter 3 should suffice. Normalization entails relatively minor additional computations during the application of a solution to new data, which must also be normalized. Normalization is determined from training data, and a description of the scale factors is part of the solution.

For classification problems, each class is represented by a separate output. For each case, a one is assigned to the correct class, and a zero to the others. For regression, the outputs are normalized along with the input data. Although the neural net is one of the simplest and most powerful representations of math solutions, obtaining the weights is a difficult task of nonlinear and iterative optimization. The goal is described as minimizing the squared error over the outputs of the training cases. Back propagation is the simplest optimization method. It has many desirable qualities, including simplicity and randomness of case training, but it is noted for very slow training that is magnified in high dimensions. The conjugate gradient method trains much faster and is often effective. If the maximum number of weights can be kept in the low thousands, possibly in conjunction with feature selection, then second-order optimization methods, such as differential equation solvers, are the most reliable training methods. Using the results of training by conjugate gradient to feed a second-order method is a particularly enticing approach that is used successfully in the experiments of Chapter 6.

III. Dimension Reduction

The effects of high data dimensions are multiplied by the structural complexity of representing hidden units. Each hidden unit is attached to all features, and each connection has an associated weight. With hundreds of features, the numbers of weights rise greatly for each additional hidden unit. Thus, the power of abstraction using intermediate concepts, as represented by hidden units, entails a substantial increase in solution complexity that is directly tied to the feature dimensions. The data-reduction techniques of Chapter 4 may dramatically reduce these dimensions and also reduce the search space for optimizing weights. Although usually advantageous, feature reduction increases the risk that the neural nets may miss some complex feature interactions.

IV. Solution Complexity

A neural net, fully connected with a single hidden layer, has an adjustable complexity. Starting with no hidden units, a linear solution, complexity is increased by enlarging the number of hidden units. In theory, complexity can be increased until all training cases are covered and the training error is zero. A near-optimum solution is found for each complexity, the solution is evaluated on test cases and the minimum-error solution is selected. In practice, the optimum fixed-complexity training solution is not always found, and training error may plateau and not decrease much with increasing complexity. Typical training configurations start at zero and two hidden units, thereafter doubling with each new increment. Training is optimized for each fixed configuration. For applications with few outputs but many features, the number of weights that must be trained is approximately the product of the number of features and hidden units. Finding a good solution typically requires the exploration of several solution complexities, usually by working up in complexity. Clearly, it is most advantageous to reduce the feature space. The more sophisticated strategies automatically adapt their configurations during training by generating and evaluating many competing architectures and pursuing the ones that evaluate best.

Because of the substantial computational costs for optimization of individual complexity solutions, a number of alternative strategies for varying complexity have been employed. The most widely followed strategy is to specify a single, moderate-to-large-complexity network, and then sample and evaluate the current solution at fixed time intervals, stopping when train or test error no longer decreases. The tendency of training is to find the most obvious weights first, and then gradually find more subtle weights that reduce error by making adjustments for fewer numbers cases. Although somewhat weaker and less controlled, the time-dependent approach can still capture the concept of variable complexity, often leading to good solutions.

V. Overall Assessment

Timing. The main drawbacks to neural net solutions are the times required for training. Neural net training, with times often measured in cpu-days or weeks, requires the greatest computational resources of any of the prediction methods described in this chapter. These computational requirements may lead to temptations of quicker but inadequate training. Careful attention must be paid to both optimized and variable-complexity training. Good training takes time. The training times for neural nets are directly affected by the number of features and cases. Reducing these dimensions can strongly reduce the computational times.

Explanatory Capabilities.   Neural nets can model arbitrarily complex functions using thousands of weights. From this perspective, the math solution provided by the net is far less explanatory than a simple linear solution. Viewed another way, neural nets are collections of simple feature weights and intermediate concepts presented in a uniform model of abstraction and final decisions. Using color presentations, selected parts of a network may be displayed. Weights are highlighted when they are positive factors for hidden units, and in turn, those hidden units are highlighted that most contribute to the determination of outputs. The key weights and hidden units may be few in number, providing satisfactory qualitative explanations of decision criteria.

Finding a Good Solution.   Neural nets balance very strong math solutions with simple, elegant architectures. They have the potential for optimal training usually not found in other prediction methods. Their training is sometimes complex and fraught with difficulties. Knowledgeable and attentive "tuners" of neural nets usually achieve excellent results that are competitive with the best results of other prediction methods.

5.2.3   Advanced Statistical Methods

The neural net representation is so clear and uniform that it has readily been embraced as everyman's complex statistics. From a traditional statistical perspective, the simplicity of representation does not outweigh the complex task of training the network. Although less widely used, analogous statistical models of regression have been developed. For example, the method of *projection pursuit* finds solutions in terms of the addition of locally linear solutions and smoothing functions. The more advanced statistical methods typically try to find solutions in modest time frames, a goal that is sometimes incompatible with obtaining the best results for big data. Unlike the neural nets, statistical methods tend to use more complex math and have more complicated training

$$c_1 = 1.004 + 0.634[f_3 - 3.3]_p - 0.631[f_3 - 1.7]_p$$
$$c_2 = 0.980 + 3.562[f_4 - 1.9]_p - 3.435[f_4 - 1.6]_p - 0.528[3.3 - f_3]_p -$$
$$8.946[f_3 - 4.9]_p[1.9 - f_4]_p + 7.793[f_3 - 5.1]_p[1.9 - f_4]_p$$
$$c_3 = -0.001 - 3.523[f_4 - 1.9]_p + 3.439[f_4 - 1.6]_p +$$
$$9.283[f_3 - 4.9]_p[1.9 - f_4]_p - 8.111[f_3 - 5.1]_p[1.9 - f_4]_p +$$
$$1.076[f_4 - 1.2]_p[5.8 - f_1]_p$$

Figure 5.3: A MARS Solution

procedures. A good example of an advanced and effective nonlinear statistical method is *MARS*, an acronym for Multiple Adaptive Regression by Splines. It combines many advanced scoring ideas from statistical research and is willing to spend some extra time searching for math solutions.

I. Solution Representation

Figure 5.3 illustrates a MARS solution for the iris data. MARS is a regression method; classification is simulated by finding a solution for each class and selecting the strongest answer for a case. For classification, one equation is described for each class. The terms involve truncated math expressions called *splines*: only the positive part of the spline expression, $[...]_p$, is used. Thus, $[f_3 - 1.7]_p$ evaluates to 0 for $f_3 < 1.7$, and to $(f_3 - 1.7)$ otherwise. Some of the terms in the iris example use second-order interactions between variables. The interactions and the truncated computations make the solutions nonlinear. The simple bracketed, linear splines take a difference between a feature and a constant, and can be increased in complexity. For instance, cubic splines, which are more complicated math functions, can be substituted for linear splines. A case is classified by plugging the case values of features into the equations and computing c_i. The class with the maximum value of c_i is the answer for a case.

The more general form of a solution is described in Equation 5.5 for two variable interactions and linear splines.

$$y = W_0 + \sum_{i=1}^{S_1} W_{1i}[s_{1i}(f_{1i} - t_{1i})]_p + \sum_{i=1}^{S_2} W_{2i} \prod_{j=1}^{2} [s_{2ij}(f_{2ij} - t_{2ij})]_p \qquad (5.5)$$

y is the continuous predicted quantity. A solution in Equation 5.5 is the sum of the following subexpressions:

- A constant value W_0

- A weighted sum of S_1 basis functions involving exactly one variable

- A weighted sum of S_2 basis functions involving interactions between two variables

W_{1i} and W_{2i} are weights associated with individual spline expressions, $[s(f - t)]_p$, where s is a plus or minus sign, f is a feature and t is the spline knot, a constant that acts as a threshold to determine when the spline expression is truncated to zero.

II. Data Preparation and Learning

MARS uses the standard spreadsheet form without normalization. The algorithm can model categorical features directly, and can cope with missing values in the training sample.

The induction task is expensive when compared to classical linear methods, but it is usually much faster than training a fully connected neural net. The search space can be great when the number of feature interactions is large. For many real-world applications, the number of predictive features is a small subset of the full set of features. Procedurally, the method is an eclectic combination of the best concepts of the logic methods with the generality of additive math solutions. These ideas include recursive partitioning, dynamic feature selection, and smoothing by spline functions. Mathematically, the objective is regression using a search for a math expression that minimizes the squared distance between correct answers and a solution's predicted values.

III. Dimension Reduction

Like the logic methods, MARS has its own dynamic feature selection techniques. Data mining with MARS is computationally expensive. When the feature space is large, preprocessing using the feature selection procedures of Chapter 4 may be helpful in reducing computational costs.

IV. Solution Complexity

The complexity of the solution is determined by the number of basis functions and feature interactions. Solution complexity is dynamically adjusted to fit the data. Upper bounds on complexity are fixed prior to training. Within these bounds, the method adjusts solution complexity to maximize predictive performance.

V. Overall Assessment

Timing. MARS typically uses less time to train than neural nets, but much more time than the classical linear classifiers or the tree methods. Constraints on the search space are given prior to training, and these affect both the computational time and the quality of solutions. Like neural net training procedures, MARS has many parameters that can be tuned based on experimentation.

Explanatory Capabilities. Statistical methods, particularly additive models, come with good visualization techniques. MARS produces solutions that are mapped into two- or three-dimensional displays. Because the critical feature interactions are directly enumerated, interpretations of solutions can be given by tracing the interacting features and weights.

Finding a Good Solution. MARS is a heuristic approach for finding potentially complex math solutions with reasonable resources. In order to induce from large samples with many cases and features, the user-specified parameters should be set carefully because they have a

substantial impact on performance. MARS seems to do best when interactions involve at most a few variables and the final model size is small.
Smaller solutions have enhanced explanatory capabilities. The method
automatically determines many solution characteristics including the
weights W_{ij}, the spline knots t_{ij} and the number of basis functions S_i.
Other parameters must be tuned, such as constraining the search to
reasonable levels by setting upper limits on the number of feature interactions.

The additive spline solutions produced by MARS usually have far
fewer math terms than those implicit in the neural net. The math may
seem less uniform and coordinated than the fully connected net. In contrast, a neural net appears to have too many weights for safe estimation.
However, in a net, all features are filtered through intermediate ab-
stractions, the hidden units, that smooth the high-dimensional feature
space and produce lower dimensions for final decisions. MARS's solution
quality is competitive with neural nets on regression applications. For
classification with discrete outputs, spline-based math solutions are less
advantageous.

5.3   Distance Solutions

In an idealized approach to prediction, a sample of cases is examined,
and a solution is found that compactly summarizes the data and gen-
eralizes to new cases. The solution is represented independently of the
training cases, which can be discarded once the solution is found. An
alternative view of prediction, seemingly well suited to high-speed computers, is table lookup. The cases are stored, and the answer for a new
case is found by looking for its entry and answer in the table. For high-
dimensional applications, the likelihood of finding an identical case in
a stored table is extremely small. The number of combinations of feature values far exceeds the number of stored cases. The underpinning
of prediction is generality to new cases, and an exact match lookup
is ineffective. Instead, distance measures are used to find the stored
cases most similar to a new case. For the k-nearest-neighbor prediction
method, k-NN, the k-nearest neighbors of a new case are determined. In
the simplest situation, the answer of the single nearest neighbor is the
answer selected for the new case.

Case	f_1	f_2	f_3	f_4	Class	Absolute Distance
1	5.1	3.5	1.4	0.2	1	6.6
...	...	...	...	...	...	...
51	7.0	3.2	4.7	1.4	2	2.1
...	...	...	...	...	...	...
141	6.7	3.1	5.6	2.4	3	2.0
...	...	...	...	...	...	...
new	5.9	3.0	5.1	1.8	3	

Table 5.1: An Example of Nearest-Neighbor Distance

I. Solution Representation

A solution for the nearest-neighbor method is comprised of three components:

- The set of stored cases

- The distance metric used to compute the distance to similar cases

- The value of k, the number of nearest neighbors to retrieve

Once the k-nearest neighbors are retrieved, their labels are examined. For classification, the class label assigned to the largest number of the k cases is selected. For regression, the average value of the k labels is the answer. Table 5.1 illustrates the computations of distance for the iris data using the single nearest neighbor. For the new case, the absolute distance from each case in the data is computed, and the new case is classified based on the class label of the closest case.

II. Data Preparation and Learning

Cases accessed by nearest-neighbor methods can be stored in standard spreadsheet form. Like data prepared for input to neural nets, the data may be normalized using the techniques of Chapter 3. This equalizes the scale for computing distance and is most effective when standard distance measures are used, such as absolute or euclidean distance.

Distance can also be computed with unequal weightings of the features, for example, a linear score where some features are given extra weight. Instead of preparing data for the standard form, more knowledgeable distance computations can automatically normalize the cases and decompose categorical features.

Training for the default nearest-neighbor method is trivial: the training cases are stored in a table. For a naive table lookup, the cases are scanned sequentially. When the number of training samples is very large, sequential storage and lookup are highly inefficient. Efficient use of standard k-NN typically requires parallel hardware. On conventional computers, dramatic improvements in performance are obtained by either presorting the cases or by clustering the cases in a hierarchical structure. Compared to other prediction methods, the reduced training time is substituted for increased times of application to new cases.

In general, the choice of a distance metric is critical to high-quality solutions. Extensive experimentation may be necessary to find a superior distance measure, negating the seeming advantages of no training for the default distance measures.

III. Dimension Reduction

Because the stored cases cover only a minor portion of the potential variations of cases, the quality of distance answers is greatly affected by noisy, nonpredictive features. Feature selection can be a very valuable tool in obtaining good performance. For some applications, it may be feasible to delete cases that do not affect overall predictive performance. Extensive experimentation may be necessary to ascertain that predictive performance is unaffected by deleted cases.

IV. Solution Complexity

The simplest complexity measure for potential solutions is measured by the number of neighbors, k, sampled by the distance measure. Starting with the single nearest neighbor, the number of neighbors is increased and error on test cases is measured. The k with the minimum error is selected. Increasing the number of stored cases tends to support larger values of k, which represent a larger sample on which to base decisions.

V. Overall Assessment

Timing. Using the standard default approach, nearest neighbors is one of the slowest ways to get answers. Using sorting, the number of comparisons can shrink from order N, the number of training cases, for the naive algorithm, to $logN$ or possibly to a constant number of comparisons independent of the size of the training sample. The algorithms for reorganizing the data are nontrivial and of complexity similar to other prediction methods. Without specialized hardware, the cost of experimentation can be quite high.

Explanatory Capabilities. Unlike the math or logic methods, distance solutions do not find generalized patterns that summarize decision criteria. All explanations are based on similarity of stored cases to a new case. When predictive performance is good, the retrieval and review of similar cases may be quite satisfactory and helpful. Taking an information retrieval approach, the nearest neighbors can be very informative, summarizing specific prior experience for similar cases.

Finding a Good Solution. The effectiveness of distance solutions is greatly enhanced by parallel machines. For big data and conventional machines, their practicality is reduced. Nearest-neighbor methods can produce excellent performance, but extensive tuning with distance measures or feature subsets may be needed. Without the extra experimental effort, performance is sometimes weak.

5.4 Logic Solutions

Like the math solutions, the logic solutions summarize the sample cases. Instead of using math operations like addition and multiplication, logic solutions are expressions that are evaluated as true or false by applying Boolean or comparative operators to the feature values. These methods are often competitive with other prediction methods and have superior explanatory characteristics.

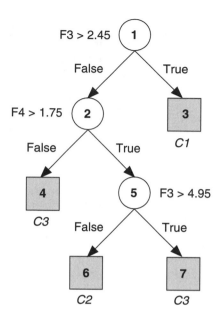

Figure 5.4: A Decision Tree

5.4.1   Decision Trees

I. Solution Representation

The decision-tree representation is the most widely used logic method, and relatively small trees are easy to understand. Figure 5.4 is a binary decision tree for the iris data. To classify a case, the root node is tested as a true-or-false decision point. Depending on the result of the test associated with the node, the case is passed down the appropriate branch, and the process continues. When a terminal node is reached, its stored value is the answer. The paths to terminal nodes are mutually exclusive.

II. Data Preparation and Learning

The tree can work directly with the standard spreadsheet form, and the values are not normalized. Some tree programs have capabilities for processing coded categorical features without explicitly preparing them as multiple true-or-false features. They also may handle missing values through surrogates.

Using training cases, the task is to determine the nodes in the tree and the tests associated with nonterminal nodes. Algorithms to perform this task generally rely on recursive partitioning of the data by picking the single best feature to separate the data and repeating the process on the subdivisions of data. The terminal nodes are assigned to the plurality class of the training cases for classification, or the median (or mean) value for regression. Within this general process, many variations are possible including binary or nonbinary trees, measures for evaluating the best feature to partition and pruning methods to reduce a tree's size.

III. Dimension Reduction

Tree induction is well suited for high-dimensional applications. It is usually the fastest nonlinear prediction method and employs dynamic feature selection. The method can take advantage of various types of data reduction including value reduction and incremental case analysis.

IV. Solution Complexity

The size of the tree, expressed as the number of terminal nodes, is a measure of the complexity of a solution. The most complex tree covers all cases in the training data. Less complex solutions are found by pruning the tree and measuring error on progressively smaller trees. There are many ways of pruning a tree, for example, by significance testing at varying levels. Most decision-tree methods provide for automatic complexity adjustment either by testing many trees of different sizes or by pruning to a fixed significance level.

V. Overall Assessment

Timing. Tree induction is fast relative to other prediction methods. For high-dimensional data, a marked slowdown in performance is caused by the repeated sorting of feature values. Presorting and possibly value reduction can greatly reduce computational time. The extra steps of complexity analysis, pruning and evaluation, are relatively small consumers of time.

Explanatory Capabilities.   The main advantage of logic-based solutions is their strong explanatory capabilities. Small trees are highly interpretable and intuitive for humans. As tree size increases, the quality of explanation decreases, reaching a point where the tree is difficult to unravel. An implied decision rule of a tree is a complete path to a terminal node. Because these rules are mutually exclusive, the size of the tree can grow much larger than the logic needed for overlapping rules. Just a single rule can combine a large number of terms—for example, more than a dozen true-or-false conditions, which greatly complicates understanding by humans.

Finding a Good Solution.   The decision tree is fast and usually produces high-quality solutions. It is an excellent choice for establishing a baseline on performance. It is not unusual to tune another method to better performance than a standard tree. To achieve better results than the tree usually requires substantial investments in time and experimentation with other prediction methods. Even then, the tree has not exhausted its performance potential because many enhancements are available, for example, limited math functions.

5.4.2   Decision Rules

Decision trees and rules are related logical representations. Decision rules are equally expressive and may be preferred because their solutions are often simpler and more intuitive. However, their induction procedures are much more complex than those for decision trees.

I. Solution Representation

If-then propositions are a routine representation for decision making with strong explanatory capabilities. The conditional part of the rule is a Boolean expression in propositional form. The conclusion is an assignment of class or value. Unlike tree paths, decision rules need not be

$$
\begin{aligned}
F3 \leq 2.45 &\quad \to \quad \text{Class} = 1 \\
F3 \leq 4.95 \wedge F4 \leq 1.7 &\quad \to \quad \text{Class} = 2 \\
\text{Otherwise} &\quad \to \quad \text{Class} = 3
\end{aligned}
$$

Figure 5.5: An Example of a Decision-Rule Solution

mutually exclusive, and some mechanism is needed for combining rules or selecting a single rule. A common technique is to order the rules, and the first satisfied rule is selected.

Each decision rule is a conjunction (AND) of true-or-false terms, and the rules are related to each other by disjunction (OR). This type of logical representation is sometimes called *disjunctive normal form*. Figure 5.5 illustrates a decision-rule solution for the iris data. The third rule is a default rule that is always satisfied. When the first two rules are not satisfied, the case is classified as Class 3.

Any decision tree can be represented as a decision-rule model in which the rules do not overlap. This can be done simply by making each path to a terminal node into a rule, where the IF part is a conjunction of the tests on the path, and the THEN part is the label of the terminal node on the path. By permitting overlaps between rules, decision-rule models are potentially simpler and more compact.

II. Data Preparation and Learning

Data preparation for the decision rules is no different than for the trees. The standard spreadsheet form is adequate, and some implementations have special mechanisms for processing categorical features without explicitly preparing them as multiple true-or-false features. Some rule-based methods require that ordered numerical features be discretized into true-or-false features covering a specific range of values. Of all the prediction methods, decision rules have the greatest potential for managing missing values because of the overlapping, disjunctive rules.

The learning objective is to determine the rules and their terms. The tasks for learning rules are similar to those for trees. A set of rules is found that covers the cases. The covering set can be induced directly in disjunctive normal form using specialized rule-induction methods, or an induced decision tree can be the starting point for further processing. Complexity is varied by pruning. The ruleset with the best test performance is selected. Because the rulesets are overlapping, most algorithms are much more complex than those for decision-tree induction. For example, the effect of pruning a single rule is not assessed independently of other rules. Some rule-induction systems incorporate iterative optimization procedures to improve and stabilize results.

Decision rules are a natural representation for knowledge stored in databases, and similar logic models, known as *association rules*, have been implemented for database systems. Predictive data mining tries to find a set of rules that covers all new cases, in effect generalizing a description of all available data for a predictive goal. This requires a detailed evaluation of the interaction of many rules and their collective predictive performance. In contrast, association rules are often evaluated independently relative to a goal, and a complete covering set for all situations is not expected. Thus a database system may be asked to find all rules, in the form of true-or-false conjunctive terms, such that a goal is met with a minimum threshold of confidence. For example, find all independent conjunctive rules having greater than 90% likelihood that the loans are repaid on time. With big data, prediction methods can also test individual rules. However, database techniques for finding association rules are more in tune with discovering opportunities and niche markets, concepts not covering the full spectrum of possibilities, but still very valuable relationships. Association rules have been extended to handle sequential relationships, such as time sequences. A constraint is added to the rules such that the associated events must occur in a time frame prior to the goal. For example, find all events that are likely to occur prior to a loan default.

III. Dimension Reduction

Rule-induction methods usually perform dynamic feature selection and operate effectively with many features. Iterative training procedures are sometimes used, increasing the number of expressions and terms that are examined far beyond the decision-tree procedures. Value reduction and smoothing can be very helpful in this environment.

IV. Solution Complexity

The total number of terms in a complete set of rules is usually taken as the measure of the complexity of a solution. Complexity is varied by pruning a covering ruleset into a series of nested rulesets until only a single rule remains. Alternative pruning strategies are also available such as pruning directly on test cases. The natural possibilities of pruning are the deletion of complete rules or individual terms. In a large ruleset, the number of rules or terms can readily number in the thousands. When the rule terms are not ordered, the evaluation of the best term to delete can be an expensive computation. In comparison, the tree-pruning computations are trivial.

Deletion of a single rule contracts coverage of cases, whereas deletion of a single term, from a rule with additional terms, expands coverage. Pruning is a relatively unstable process that may require some refinement or optimization of a pruned ruleset, particularly when the ruleset is composed of relatively few rules or terms.

V. Overall Assessment

Timing. Inducing decision rules is computationally more expensive than tree induction. Value reduction and presorting are important time-savers, particularly for iterative procedures. For low-prevalence classification, timings are quite good even for very large samples. As the sample size increases, the size of the covering set usually increases, sometimes to very large covering sets of thousands of rules. For some rule-induction programs, the time to find a solution may greatly increase because effective pruning or optimization is far slower for decision rules than trees. Tuning parameters can also have important effects on timing. Although the rule representation may have potential advantages over the tree for explanation and predictive performance, complex procedures are needed to achieve potential gains.

Explanatory Capabilities. Rules have strong explanatory capabilities that are intuitively satisfying for humans. When rules begin to have excessive conditions, or when the number of rules is large, the explanatory power of the ruleset is somewhat compromised. To maintain its explanatory power, the prediction algorithms may spend extra time searching for solutions of reduced complexity that are also highly predictive.

Finding a Good Solution.   Decision-rule solutions are often found that exceed the performance of decision trees and are far more inter-pretable and compact. The advantage for decision rules is mostly found when a modestly complex solution is the most predictive. For multiclass applications and complex solutions, decision-tree performance is often difficult to exceed without great tuning of the parameters for rule in-duction. Overall predictive performance is often competitive with the math and distance solutions.

5.5   What Do the Answers Mean?

The traditional approach to abstracting and comparing different types of solutions is by geometric analogy. For example, the archetypal de-scription of a linear discriminant is given in Figure 5.6, where a line, or hyperplane, separates idealized classes.

These idealized descriptions play a less active role in understanding the more variable representations and solutions of high-dimensional data. Given enough data, modern methods are capable of reshaping themselves and their solutions by using simple, basic units to fit data. Geometric descriptions of these basic units, such as the rectangles used by logic methods fitting to the data, are of great practical help in under-standing the potential capabilities of a method, particularly in compar-ison to other methods.

For big data, evaluation of results is simple and immediate. If predic-tive performance is the sole criterion for comparing proposed solutions, then no further explanation is needed. The computer is a handy tool to support this view.

People usually look for help in understanding a solution. They want to know why an answer is given. Various visualization techniques have been developed to give an overall picture of a solution. For example, some regression solutions can be transformed into two-dimensional plots

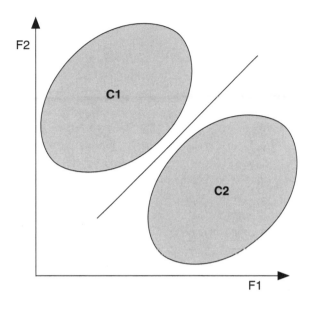

Figure 5.6: Linear Discriminant for an Idealized Situation

of an aggregate x, the inputs, versus y, the outputs. Many useful graphical aids have been developed, particularly for the math solutions.

In an age of big data and flexible prediction methods that generate many solutions of different complexity, the meaning of solutions is more difficult to express. Generally, explanations of answers follow the three categories of methods:

- Math answers are explained by the positive and negative influences of their weights.

- Distance answers are explained by offering a few cases that are most similar to a new case.

- Logic answers are explained by the rules that are invoked for a new case.

5.5.1   Is It Safe to Edit Solutions?

Solutions induced from data can be far from optimal, and samples may be compromised or biased. The application experts always have the option of using superior knowledge to select and modify proposed solutions. The potential for editing solutions is related to the interpretability of their answers. Weights can be very difficult to manually adjust, particularly when their number is large. The linear solutions are relatively transparent and can be examined as collections of positive and negative factors. It is not unreasonable to manually raise or lower weights of key features and move the decision in a particular direction. For nonlinear solutions, the interactions may be more complex, and the consequences of editing weights more uncertain. A simpler decision is to delete features that appear marginal or are less desirable based on other considerations, such as the expense of measuring them. Decisions can be made from personal knowledge and experience, but their validity should also be objectively tested on cases.

The logic solutions are ripe for manual editing. For simple decision trees, it is not unusual to consider replacing a small subtree with an alternative subtree, especially when the features are categorical. A more likely decision is to prune a tree further, when a slight gain in predictive performance for a larger tree is outweighed by less satisfactory explanations. For decision rules, the temptation for manual revision and tweaking is always present. The rules are not mutually exclusive and have consequences relative to other rules, but they also appear to have independent meaning. For example, it's easy to take a single rule from a much larger ruleset and add a new condition to the rule that restricts its invocation. No matter how intuitive a proposed revision, empirical testing validates modifications. Sometimes an application expert will propose a complete solution that is expressed in the same logical representation. In a sense, the human and machine compete for acceptance of solutions. Big data will make it more difficult for human experts to update rulesets and fit cases that do support current solutions. But it is quite reasonable to combine the strengths of man and machine. For example, a physician may have knowledge of current medical laboratory testing and may not be willing to diverge greatly from a standard small set of tests and features. However, the numerical thresholds for decision rules are less obvious and better determined by a machine looking at historical records.

The distance solutions derive their explanations from examples of similar cases. A solution is expressed in terms of a distance measure and a warehouse of cases. Baseline solutions for nearest-neighbor methods are usually obtained using one of the default measures, such as euclidean distance. However, true devotees of this approach have sometimes developed high-performance solutions using highly tuned distance measures. These measures are manually adjusted, but require extensive empirical evaluation. Very effective solutions have also been found by augmenting a statistical sample with prototypical cases developed by human experts. Is it possible to induce solutions without cases? Even for the distance solutions, the answer is yes. Given a set of features with enough knowledge and perseverance, a set of cases can be composed. Using this "case-based reasoning" approach, successful solutions have been found by eventually mixing objectively sampled cases with subjective cases composed by experts.

5.6 Which Solution Is Preferable?

Among the key factors that influence the choice of prediction method are predictive performance, explanation capabilities and the expected effort to achieve that performance. Outside of research circles, a single method is usually selected and all results are obtained with this method. Traditionally, the linear solution has been the favored route. Classical linear methods have good performance on moderate samples, give reasonable explanations and the effort is very modest. For big data, concerns are more likely to arise about using such a rigid representation that often continues to work well but is sometimes uncompetitive with the more flexible alternatives.

The logical contender for succession to the classical linear approach is the decision tree. Predictive performance is usually competitive, as are the explanations. With modern computers, even for big data, the computational requirements are reasonable, and the effort to obtain these solutions is modest. The decision tree gives good performance across a broad spectrum of applications, both classification and regression, but it often loses to other methods that are highly tuned for specific applications.

The baseline performance of the decision tree, or perhaps a linear solution, helps greatly in tuning one of the other methods. The distance solutions can be desirable, particularly for information retrieval applications, where similarity to other cases is an essential ingredient in the solution. The nearest-neighbor methods may require extensive experimentation to achieve the best performance, and competitive benchmarks can indicate minimum goals for performance. It's not unusual for distance solutions to start with poor performance using default settings and gradually build to solutions that yield superior results.

The decision rules are related to trees, but they may express more intuitive explanations and sometimes have superior predictive performance. The effort is much greater, and the tree's baseline performance is invaluable. The greatest effort is for the neural nets whose representation is so uniform and simple that it has revolutionized math methods. Unlike the other methods, solutions can be theoretically optimal. In practice, it's easy to go wrong. For regression, an advanced statistical method like MARS can produce impressive math solutions for less effort than neural net optimization.

Although the wiser approach is to keep an eye on the competition, the typical approach is to use a single method. It's just too hard to be the master of different programs with different data requirements and parameters. A single method can be selected based on the factors outlined above. However, when predictive performance is the sole goal, and effort and explanation are of lesser consequence, a combination of several methods or solutions may give the best results.

5.7   Combining Different Answers

Big data can potentially support complex solutions, and candidate solutions are readily evaluated on large numbers of test cases. Finding solutions with the best predictive performance may entail extra experiments and nonstandard representations.

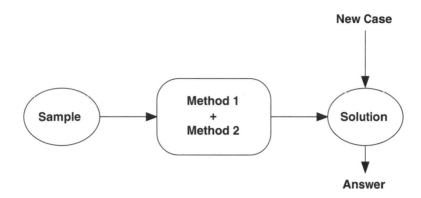

Figure 5.7: Combining Complementary Prediction Methods

5.7.1   Multiple Prediction Methods

One approach to better predictive performance is to combine solutions from two different representations. Figure 5.7 illustrates this approach where complementary prediction methods that have some potential weaknesses combine to form a stronger solution. For example, the logic methods are unable to score or add, and linear methods cannot find complex solutions. A linear discriminant can first be determined, and its decisions for each class may be used as additional features for a decision tree. Similarly, a regression tree may be induced with combined methods. For each terminal in a tree, predictions of a constant value are made. Alternatively, the value for a new case may be determined by the case's nearest neighbor among the training cases in the corresponding terminal node.

The combined approach of Figure 5.7 integrates two different representations into a single solution. This type of solution often maintains good explanatory capabilities at the expense of a complicated prediction algorithm. A simpler "stacking" approach to prediction, illustrated in Figure 5.8, independently finds solutions from several different prediction methods and representations. The answers of the prediction methods are combined in a weighted fashion—for example, 50% of the tree answer, 30% of a neural net answer, and 20% of a nearest-neighbor

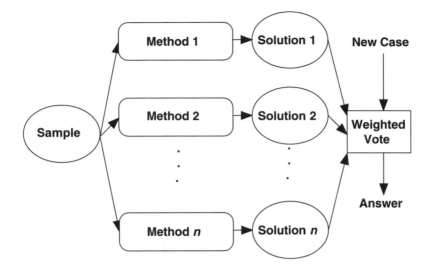

Figure 5.8: Weighted Combinations of Independent Prediction Methods

method. These simple weights should be tuned, but results can surpass any of those for a single method.

5.7.2 Multiple Samples

Averaging or voting solutions over many random samples is described in Section 4.6.3 as a technique for case reduction when a prediction program's capacity is exceeded. Because average solutions have little variance, predictive performance may increase, sometimes dramatically. When a potential sample is huge, effectively infinite, most prediction methods can do much better by averaging or voting solutions from many samples of size N than by finding a solution for a single size N sample.

Even when the training set is finite, and well within the capacity of a prediction program, averaging solutions can decrease error. Given a training set with N cases, simulated samples can be drawn from it, and the solutions taken for these samples averaged or voted. How are the samples drawn? In the simplest approach, bootstrap samples are taken. For bootstrapping, N cases are randomly selected with replacement; cases in the simulated sample may repeat. Each case is weighted equally: the probability of selecting a specific next case is $1/N$. Unlike sampling from a general population, here a simulated sample repeats many cases, with an expected 63% unique cases. Prediction methods that can cover the training cases with little error will likely benefit from averaged bootstrap solutions because of the reduced variance. For methods with low variance, such as linear or nearest-neighbor methods, bootstrap averaging usually does not improve results over the single, full-sample solution.

How many different samples and solutions are needed? When test cases are available, incremental progress in predictive performance can be monitored. Error may not decrease monotonically, but a trend in decreasing error should be noticed over increasing numbers of samples until a limit is reached. For bootstrap samples, most of the reduction in error can be obtained with 10 samples. Over 50 samples, further improvement is not likely. For samples that are substantially smaller than the available training set, many more samples need be drawn to achieve minimum error. Still, large gains may be encountered with as few as 10 samples.

The samples are drawn from cases in the data warehouse, or new cases may be collected to form a sample whose solution may be averaged with the others. The samples are drawn randomly with equal probability, or new cases arrive randomly. Adaptive sampling, which doesn't sample cases equally, is often superior and less biased. Cases having large error for current solutions are drawn with increased frequency. For each case in the full training set, a record is kept of current solution performance. Instead of randomly selecting cases with probability $1/N$, where N is the full sample size, cases are selected with probability p_i, the relative probability of error for case i. The higher the error, the more likely the case is selected. The value of p_i need not be an optimal error computation. One approximation is given in Equation 5.8, where e_i is the sum of error for case i. Each solution is independently tested on case i, and the cumulative error over all independent solutions is recorded in e_i. A case with many errors becomes a prime target for inclusion in a new sample, and for classification problems, Equation 5.7 may be preferable to Equation 5.6.

$$perf_i = e_i \tag{5.6}$$

$$perf_i = 1 + e_i^3 \tag{5.7}$$

$$p_i = \frac{perf_i}{\sum_{j=1}^{N} perf_j} \tag{5.8}$$

For a finite training set of size N, p_i should be computed over the full training set. If this is not too large, then samples of size N are best. Smaller sample sizes are also very effective, often reaching the same predictive performance, but with many more samples. Although adaptive sampling usually surpasses the performance of bootstrap sampling, more samples are often needed to reach its predictive limit.

Some training sets may be so large that they can be considered infinite relative to samples of size N: few if any cases will repeat even when all size N samples are pooled. A sample drawn from completely new cases can also be considered drawn from an infinite sample. For an infinite set of cases, p_i, can be computed over M new cases, $M > N$, and a sample of size N is drawn from these cases based on p_i.

The decision tree is an excellent candidate for averaging or voting. Tree induction is fast, and single-sample solutions are often good but non-optimal. A covering decision tree has little bias and high variance. The variance may be greatly reduced by averaging or voting. Where feasible, results for a combined approach should always be compared to those for a single solution. Performance gains from any approach to combined solutions must be carefully weighed against the additional complexity of solutions. The apparent and practical complexity of an averaged solution is very large because many solutions must be retained to obtain an answer. However, the averaged solution has a conceptual complexity similar to a single constituent solution.

5.8 Bibliographic and Historical Remarks

The basic concepts of classification and regression, which apply to all prediction methods, are discussed in [Friedman, 1995]. Many of the key prediction methods, and the techniques for practical evaluation of performance, are reviewed in [Weiss and Kulikowski, 1991]. The classical statistical methods are clearly described in [James, 1985]. Excellent reviews of neural nets and their relationships to statistics are in [Ripley, 1993; Ripley, 1994; Cheng and Titterington, 1994]. MARS is described in [Friedman, 1991]. An example of an adaptive training strategy, genetic algorithms, for self-adjusting neural net architectures is given in [Miller, Todd and Hedge, 1989]. A collection of key pattern-recognition papers on nearest-neighbor methods can be conveniently accessed in [Dasarathy, 1991]. The related case-based reasoning methods, which mix both machine methods and manual descriptions of cases, are described in [Kolodner, 1993]. Rule-based methods are presented in [Weiss and Indurkhya, 1993]. The related concepts of association rules and their implementation in database systems are discussed in [Agrawal, Mannila, Srikant, Toivonen and Verkamo, 1996].

Stacking is formally described in [Wolpert, 1992]. Combined representations of logic methods for regression are discussed in [Weiss and Indurkhya, 1995]. The bootstrap form of combination, known as *bagging*, or *bootstrap aggregates*, is described in [Breiman, 1996a]. The adaptive resampling combination, *arcing*, is presented in [Breiman, 1996b], and is an unweighted variation of the *boosting* algorithm of [Freund, 1995; Freund and Schapire, 1996]. Results of voting solutions on adaptively simulated samples show impressive gains, leading to potentially near-optimal solutions for predictive data-mining applications [Quinlan, 1996]. An alternative to fully automated prediction is the belief or Bayesian network, that combines man-made architectures, like expert-specified decision trees, with probabilities induced from cases [Heckerman, 1996]. A number of data-mining tools are available over the web. A selective directory of data-mining software can be found by following the links at www.data-miner.com.

6

What's Best for Data Reduction and Mining?

The big data have been transformed to standard format, and the software toolbox is loaded with techniques to mine data. Two types of tools have been discussed:

- Data-reduction techniques

- Prediction methods

Because data reduction is much faster than data modeling, the data are filtered to narrow the search space of the prediction methods. However, the reduction methods make assumptions that potentially could degrade results. These tools have been selected because historically they have a record of positive results on numerous real-world applications. In this chapter, we apply the prediction methods and data-reduction techniques to big data. Instead of relying solely on the historical record, empirical comparisons are made of the different data-reduction techniques. These techniques are then matched to the prediction methods to see which combinations work best.

The comparisons of different approaches to data reduction and mining should help us gain experience in picking the right tools for the job. Here, the evaluation is based on formal scientific principles. In Chapter 7, the artistic contributions needed for real-world applications are also factored into the data-mining picture.

Our scientific assessment of competing approaches is based on the empirical results of applying the methods to several large spreadsheets. There are three types of dimensions: features, values and cases. Various methods and techniques are evaluated by fixing all characteristics except for the one that is varied. Each data-reduction method can be evaluated over many prediction methods for quality of results, solution complexity and computational timings. Later, combinations of techniques are considered.

6.1   Let's Analyze Some Real Data

The environment for this comparative study is a controlled laboratory setting where different methods are applied to the same data and evaluated under identical conditions. This scenario is somewhat artificial and simplifies the real-world conditions necessary for best results. For this study, the goals are to compare and evaluate the different tools that are available, assessing their strengths and weaknesses, and demonstrating their potential for effective data mining. Complete or optimal solutions for the applications need not be obtained. The results tell us about trends that have been found for these applications. If these applications are typical of other applications, then the generality of the conclusions is supported. They are especially valid when the results can be related to the assumptions made by the techniques. The results demonstrate potential effectiveness, not absolute winners.

Although the experiments are carefully controlled, they have real-world consequences in two important ways:

- The data are obtained from significant real-world applications.

- Problem solving simulates the real-world application of data-mining methods.

How are data-reduction techniques evaluated? Data-reduction techniques are filters for prediction methods. These filters attempt to reduce dimensions by deleting nonessential information. Hence, their usefulness can be assessed by studying their impact on the prediction methods. This suggests an experimental protocol. The data-reduction methods are compared by examining the predictive performance of solutions obtained from prediction methods operating on reduced data.

Performance is determined by testing on a large set of independent cases. Most prediction methods induce many solutions, and the best one is selected. The best one is usually judged by test case performance. For example, most methods generate variable-complexity solutions, and only one of these is eventually selected. For greater scientific objectivity, a second test set of completely hidden test cases may be set aside to provide an unbiased evaluation. Three different sets of cases are maintained for each application:

- Train: These data are used for training. They represent the complete pool of data available to the reduction techniques and the prediction methods.

- Test1: These test data can be used by the reduction techniques and prediction methods to select from alternative solutions. If too much tuning is done, the error estimates can be somewhat optimistic. In our experiments, little tuning is done, and generally these cases are used only for selecting from different complexity solutions.

- Test2: These are independent test cases, completely hidden from all reduction and prediction methods. They are used solely for evaluating error of solutions that have already been selected by the prediction methods.

With an expectation of big data, it is easy to envision the feasibility of these divisions of data. From a practical perspective, with careful controls on the type of testing that is performed, it is more likely that a single test set will be used. In a study, greater circumspection is advised, particularly when multiple prediction methods are compared. For accurate selection and evaluation, test sets should number in the thousands of cases, with greater numbers of cases for low-prevalence applications.

All summaries of results, including graphs, use error on the Test2 cases. Error is measured as error rates for classification and mean absolute distance for regression. Because most of the data are proprietary, prevalences and the real errors are not disclosed. Instead, relative errors are employed; they are particularly advantageous for pairwise comparisons.

Data from seven different applications are analyzed. The samples of cases for these applications are divided into these three subsets. The

Dataset	Cases			Features		Class
	Train	**Test1**	**Test2**	**Num.**	**Type**	
Medical	2079	501	522	33	Num+Binary	2
Telecom	62414	34922	34592	23	Num+Binary	2
Media	7133	3512	3672	87	Num	2
Control	2061	685	685	22	Num	Real
Sales	10779	3591	6156	127	Num+Binary	3
Service	4826	2409	2412	215	Binary	2
Noise	20000	5000	5000	100	Num	2

Table 6.1: Data Dimensions

dimensions of the seven datasets are summarized in Table 6.1. Descriptions of these applications, including the details of the actual data-mining steps taken to solve these problems, are discussed in Chapter 7. Here, the focus is on the study of data reduction under controlled laboratory conditions. The dimensions of these datasets are summarized below:

1. Medical: Of the 33 features, most are real-valued numbers. Two of the features have more than 350 distinct values. The positive class has a prevalence of less than 10%. Of the seven applications, this is the smallest sample, and the number of cases is only moderately large. The number of test cases is modest, but is somewhat compensated by the desirability of a low-complexity solution. The prevalence of the small class is relatively low, and it is known that the features are weak. False-negative errors are less worrisome than false positives. Balancing all these factors led to the random division of cases in the proportions described in Table 6.1.

2. Telecom: One of the features has over 8,000 distinct training values. Two other features have over 150 distinct values, and for all other features, the number of distinct values is less than 50. The prevalence of the positive class is low. The data are time-stamped and comprise several months of information. The training and test

data are sampled from fixed time periods. The test data are obtained from the most recent time period.

3. Media: The number of features is relatively large, but the features have few distinct values. No feature has more than 55 values. The prevalence of the positive class is less than 2%.

4. Control: This is a regression problem. The dependent variable ranged from -35 to $+49$ with a median of 0. All the features have many values, with a dozen of them having more than 600 different values. Many of the data-reduction techniques are specifically designed for classification problems. In applying some methods to this dataset, the dataset is treated as a two-class problem, with the positive class consisting of cases with non-negative values of the output variable. These "pseudo-classes" are created only for data reduction. The regression task is later performed on the reduced data.

5. Sales: There are three classes with prevalences of 35%, 19% and 46%, respectively. Two of the features individually have over 5,000 distinct values. Each of more than 40 of the features has over 2,000 unique values. The predicted class labels are from the most recent quarterly time period, and the features are measured from time periods prior to the class period. The train and test cases are divided randomly.

6. Service: All the features are binary. The most difficult dimension is the large number of features. Another difficulty is a class prevalence of less than 1%.

7. Noise: This is an artificial noise dataset. All feature values are random numbers from zero to one, recorded to two decimal places. Thus, all features have a maximum of 101 distinct values. The class label of each case is assigned randomly to produce a positive class with a prevalence of 25.0%.

These datasets vary widely in dimensions, exhibiting forms of high dimensions over a range of prevalences, feature types and error. Six of these are taken from commercial applications, and the seventh is added to cover an extreme, though common situation: nonpredictive data. Data, big or small, may contain no useful predictive information, and even the strongest prediction program should quickly recognize the futility of mining.

6.2   The Experimental Methods

The methods discussed in Chapters 4 and 5 are representative data-mining tools, and have excellent track records. Most methods have parameters that can be tuned for optimal performance on an application. For this study, settings for these parameters are fixed. Based on experience in other applications, these default settings should give reasonable results on a wide range of problems. Although the results are not necessarily optimal for a given prediction method, the relative effectiveness of data reduction can be determined.

Recall that there are three dimensions to consider: cases, features and values. Here are the reduction methods used for each of these dimensions:

- Case subsampling: Six percentages of the training sample are used in the experiments: 10, 20, 33, 50, 67 and 100. For each percentage, the cases are randomly selected and used for prediction.

- Feature selection: These are the methods that are used in the experiments:

  - *Step:* The stepwise, forward and backward, feature selection method. A significance threshold of 4.0 is used.

  - *Signif:* A simple test of independent feature significance. A threshold of 2.0 standard errors is used to test if the mean value of a feature is significantly different across classes.

  - *BAB:* The optimal branch-and-bound feature subset selection method. The best 15 features are selected. When the number of features is in the hundreds, this method usually needs great computational resources. The stepwise heuristic selection method is used as a preprocessor to bring the number of features to less than 60 before invoking the optimal subset selection method.

- *PCA:* The principal component analysis method. The principal components are selected that account for a larger-than-average proportion of the variance. Typically, this results in far fewer features than specified in the original feature space.

- *Tree:* The covering tree selects the features. For ties, features already selected by the tree are given preference. This usually reduces the number of features in the covering tree.

• Value reduction: The following methods are examined:

- *Round:* The simple round-off method described in Chapter 4 is applied to the values of each feature. The final data are reduced to at most 50 distinct values per feature. With binary rounding to a maximum of 50 values, the actual number of values per feature ranges between 25 and 50.

- *K-Means:* The k-means clustering procedure is applied to all values of a feature. The values are fitted to 50 bins. Each bin is represented by its median value.

- *Entropy:* Class information is used to bin the values where class entropy is minimized. The number of bins is 25, and each bin is represented by its median value. The hypothesis is that the class information might be able to reduce the number of classes beyond the k-means clustering method.

- *Inc-Entropy:* While clustering by class entropy uses a prespecified number of bins, an incremental approach gradually adds bins until there is an insignificant gain in entropy. In these experiments, a gain for entropy of less than 1% is the threshold for stopping. This procedure usually results in far fewer bins, typically less than 5. Therefore, the boundary values of the bins are used, not the medians.

The application of a reduction method with fixed parameter values should yield good results, but not necessarily the best. For best performance, each method can be individually tuned to the application. But based on prior experience, the default parameter values are reasonable and have given good results over diverse applications. The experimental design is geared for controlled comparisons of techniques for data reduction, where the results are evaluated under identical conditions with or without the use of reduction techniques.

Some selected combinations of the reduction methods are also examined. In general, the order of combination for different types of data reduction is first value reduction, then feature selection, and finally case subsampling.

The reduced data are provided as input to the prediction methods. Methods are applied from the three general categories described in Chapter 5: (a) math, (b) distance and (c) logic methods. Here are the prediction methods used in the comparisons:

- Rule: An iterative rule-induction method is used. This implementation presorts feature values and can take advantage of value reduction. Weakest-link pruning is used to induce solutions of varying complexities. This method is applied to all the variations of reduced data.

- Tree: A binary-tree induction program is used that presorts feature values and has special capabilities for value reduction. Variable-complexity solutions are generated by pruning at different, fixed-significance levels. The tree-induction program is applied to all the different versions of reduced data.

- LDA: The classical, statistical linear discriminant and regression models are used. The types of data reduction matched to this method are feature selection and case subsampling.

- Neural net: An enhanced neural network procedure is used to train single-layer, back-propagation neural networks. The network is trained by a conjugate gradient method whose results are then passed to a full second-order training method. Solutions are induced for 0, 2, 5, 10 and 20 hidden units, and the best model is selected based on performance on the selection test cases, Test1. Value reduction is of limited interest for a neural network representation and is not used. All training runs in this study are for a minimum of one cpu-day on a high-end DEC Alpha processor. Nets with fewer hidden units are trained first. As complexity increases, training continues at least until the training error is reduced below the error of a less complex network on the same data. Training also continued when the test error indicates a decreasing trend. Some net training times exceeded four cpu-days. The errors measured for other prediction methods are supplementary cross-checks on the effectiveness of net training.

- kNN: This is the k-nearest-neighbor procedure using euclidean distance. Performance is measured for $k = 1$, 5, 11 and 25, and the best value of k is selected using the Test1 cases. All variations of data reduction are tried for this method.

- MARS: This is an advanced spline-based statistical model for regression. It is used for the control application with default parameter settings.

6.3   The Empirical Results

Data-reduction techniques feed data to the prediction methods, and their comparative performances are valuable for studying data reduction. A reduction technique may be evaluated over different datasets and varying prediction methods. For a given prediction method and dataset, the *baseline* performance of a prediction method is defined as the predictive performance obtained by training on all the training data without any data reduction. Performance is measured by the error on the hidden evaluation cases, Test2.

The baseline can be used to compare the effects of the data-reduction techniques. The identical experimental conditions are used to train and evaluate a reduced dataset and the baseline. The only difference between the baseline and the reduced variation is that reduced data are substituted for the full data. Equation 6.1 describes the relative error of a reduction method in terms of the error on the reduced data and the baseline data. This measure of relative error is our principal measure of the effectiveness of a reduction technique.

$$RelativeError_{rm} = \frac{Error_{rd}}{Error_{base}} \qquad (6.1)$$

The relative error is measured for a constant prediction method. If the relative error is less than one, the data reduction is very useful for a prediction method and improves performance. A value greater than one indicates that the data reduction gives weaker performance than using all of the data. Values not much greater than one usually imply effective data reduction because data reduction greatly accelerates the induction process, with little or no loss in predictive performance. By examining relative error trends of a reduction strategy across many prediction methods and different datasets, its effectiveness can be assessed.

6.3.1 Significance Testing

Relative error is a pairwise comparison of the error for the reduced and baseline solutions. Using two independent test sets, a measure of the significance of the difference in mean error can be obtained from the standard pairwise test of Equation 2.2. Error estimates for Test1, the test set used for selection, may be slightly optimistic. However, comparing the average test results for Test1 and Test2, over all methods and datasets, suggests a very small bias in Test1 results. An approximate measure of significance can be found by averaging the significance results for the two ways that the test sets can be paired. The average may balance any biases of Test1, and the approximate significance of results at two standard errors is easily computed. For the rare event where a difference in mean error moved in opposite directions for the two comparisons, no significant difference is concluded.

In all graphs of this chapter, points that are significantly different in error are indicated by enclosing the point in a box. The significance test is the average of the two paired tests on Test1 and Test2. The magnitude of error that is significant varies across applications depending on sample size and the disparities in error for the two test sets.

6.4 So What Did We Learn?

The first set of experiments examine the effectiveness of data-reduction techniques. Different data-reduction methods are compared and contrasted on these applications. Three types of techniques are evaluated: feature selection, value reduction and case subsampling.

Dataset	Total	Step	Signif	PCA	Tree	Tree-Prune
Medical	33	10	20	12	31	18
Telecom	23	12	21	9	23	21
Media	87	47	51	27	25	10
Control	22	4	20	2	19	11
Sales	127	39	108	43	98	93
Service	215	19	134	86	32	3
Noise	100	4	4	48	100	100

Table 6.2: Data Reduction by Feature Selection

6.4.1 Feature Selection

Before gauging the effectiveness of feature selection techniques, let's ask this question: for each reduction technique and application, what is the extent of the data reduction? To contrast with other techniques, the relatively costly optimal branch-and-bound strategy, BAB, has been restricted to a fixed-dimension search for the best 15 features. For the remaining feature selection methods, the number of selected features is shown in Table 6.2. The total number of features is also shown for comparison. Except for the PCA features, which are transformed by linearly combining the original features, all other methods do a subset selection. The PCA feature reduction is comparable in terms of dimensions, but it generates new features that are amalgams of the original feature set.

For most procedures, the number of selected features is controlled by parameters such as significance levels. For two of the applications, telecom and noise, the tree method does not reduce the feature space. Covering trees can be pruned at varying significance levels comparable to the other feature selection methods. On the noise dataset, the stepwise method correctly deduces that most of the features are noise, whereas the covering tree selects many more features. The same effect occurs on the sales data. Generally, the stepwise method has the greatest impact on reducing the original feature space, while the effect of the covering tree is application dependent, having little feature reduction when there is considerable noise in the feature space. Using a covering tree is very conservative. Pruning the tree can countervail the effects of noise. As illustrated in Table 6.2, additional feature reduction is achieved using a tree and a modest amount of pruning, but the effect of a default significance level is more variable for trees than for methods that reason with mean values and variance. An independent significance test on mean values to separate out useful features usually reduces the feature space less drastically than most methods except when the features are clearly irrelevant as in the noise data. The extent of data reduction for most of the methods can be adjusted by setting a single parameter. Using a default setting usually gives good results. However, in practice, modest tuning of this parameter, by training on a random subset of cases and testing on independent cases, may be best for balancing predictive performance and the extent of feature reduction.

The critical test of feature selection is its performance measured by relative error, not the size of the feature subset. If a method keeps all the original features, such as the tree does for the relatively small feature space of the telecom data, there is no difference from the baseline. In many scenarios, feature selection has a considerable impact on performance. This impact is especially evident for a prediction method that does not incorporate dynamic feature selection. For example, Figures 6.1 and 6.2 show the trend for nearest-neighbor and neural network methods. In general, the relative errors are mostly less than one, demonstrating that generally feature selection is helpful for prediction methods that have no direct internal feature selection. For kNN, the error rates on reduced data are typically lower or the same as the baseline. This is especially true for the service data, which have 215 features. By transforming the data into the principal component features before applying nearest neighbors, the error rate is reduced by as much as 20%. The worst predictive performance is for the media data where selecting the best 15 features with optimal subset selection, BAB, gives 20% weaker performance. But the overall trend is that feature selection is very useful for kNN.

The trend for the neural networks is similar. The high relative error for the neural solution based on the principal components of the service data is worth noting. This application has only Boolean features, and the transformed feature space with continuous values is less effective than the original space consisting of inputs with binary values. The same transformation is effective for kNN, suggesting the need to match

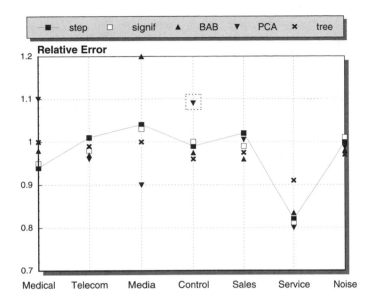

Figure 6.1: Feature Selection for Nearest Neighbors

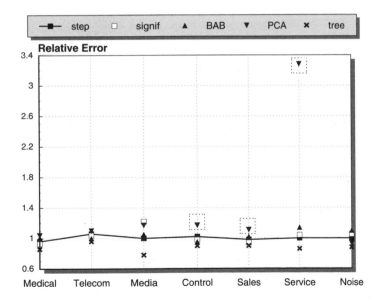

Figure 6.2: Feature Selection for Neural Nets

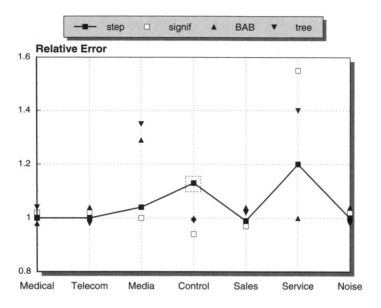

Figure 6.3: Feature Selection for Rule Learning

a data-reduction strategy to a prediction method. The great advantage of feature selection for neural networks is the vastly reduced training times without any major loss in performance. The results suggest that while tree-based selection and stepwise heuristic feature selection often have an edge, the other methods are effective.

Are these feature selection techniques also useful as filters for prediction methods that do dynamic feature selection? In principle, such preprocessing is unnecessary for methods like rule or tree induction. As shown in Figure 6.3 for rules (the results for trees are similar), these feature selection methods can help logic methods. However, the results do suggest that these prediction methods may need extra testing and tuning for best feature selection. For the logic methods, it is generally preferable to maintain a large set of features. The method's own dynamic feature selection techniques are effective without filters. In addition, value reduction can greatly reduce dimensions for the logic methods.

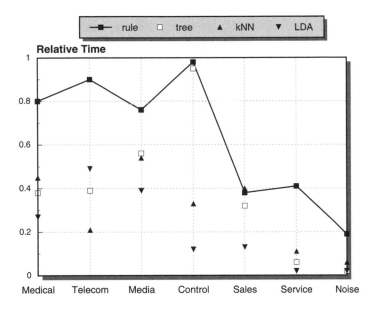

Figure 6.4: Speedups for Stepwise Feature Selection

The impact of feature selection in speeding up learning is illustrated in Figure 6.4, which plots the relative time taken by a few representative prediction methods, when the heuristic stepwise feature selection procedure is used to preselect the most relevant features. The times are plotted relative to the time taken to compute the baseline. Relative times less than one represent speedups. The trend of faster learning times is consistent for all methods when the stepwise technique is used as a preprocessor. The magnitude of the speedup is greatest for prediction methods that usually use all the features in a solution. This, coupled with the relative error results, suggests that feature selection methods are generally effective in reducing data dimensions.

6.4.2 Value Reduction

Value reduction can considerably speed up logic learning. Figures 6.5 and 6.6 describe the results of different types of value reductions. The

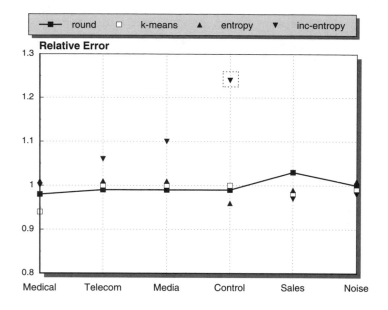

Figure 6.5: Value Reduction for Rule Learning

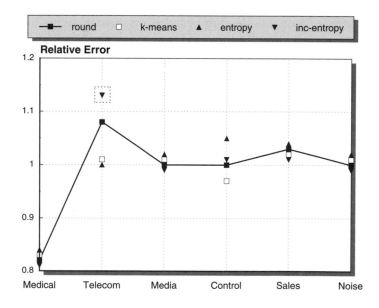

Figure 6.6: Value Reduction for Tree Learning

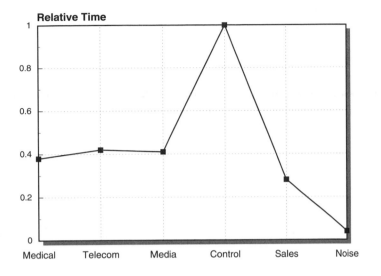

Figure 6.7: Speedups with Entropy-Based Value Reduction

service dataset has only binary features and is not used for these comparisons. All of these value-reduction techniques use a bin model for value reduction. The default maximum numbers of values provide different degrees of substantial smoothing. The incremental entropy procedure attempts to guess the best cutoffs, while the other methods have moderate numbers of bins. For these smoothing techniques, only the training data are smoothed, and test cases are not changed. The results show that smoothing using the default maximum values generally is effective. Sometimes there is a small loss relative to the baseline, and occasionally there is a gain. Although not performed in this study, tuning the smoothing technique and prediction method on a modest random subset of training and test cases may improve results. The incremental entropy method sharply reduces the number of values and does moderately well, but has the greatest risk of performance degradation.

The results of value reduction in speeding up learning are described in Figure 6.7, which plots the relative time taken by the tree-induction methods, when entropy bins are used to reduce the number of values. The times are plotted relative to the time taken to compute the baseline.

Value reduction may substantially reduce the time of computation. The actual reduction is dependent on several factors. If most of the features have fewer than the maximum threshold for reduction, value reduction will have little effect. If reduction is too great, the method may need to grow a larger covering tree or ruleset. The extra smoothing may sometimes improve predictive performance, but may not decrease run times. For reasonable default settings, the gains from value reduction are usually great in terms of timing, particularly when there are real-valued values for many features.

6.4.3 Subsampling or All Cases?

With big data, a key question is whether all the cases are needed to get the best answer. Perhaps the same quality of answer can be found when fewer cases are used for learning. The number of cases needed to find the best answer depends on the complexity of the concepts implicit in the data. When too few cases are used, there is a chance that some concepts will not be found. However, some prediction methods may be somewhat unstable, and with more data, they may search in unproductive areas, leading to weaker answers than would be found for fewer cases. For the applications of this study, we can look back and ask whether the best answer is always found with the complete set of cases.

Experiments are performed on random subsamples of the training data. Prediction methods are applied to various fixed fractions of the data, and the best solution for each subsample is found by using the selection test cases, Test1. For each prediction method, these solutions, including the 100% solution, are compared and evaluated using the evaluation test cases, Test2. The percentage of cases for the best solution is then recorded. The objective is to determine where the best answer lies and whether it is found consistently with 100% of the cases. In the real world, this form of analysis may be unrealistic, and reasonable percentages of cases can vary greatly with the sample size. However, this retrospective analysis can summarize the experience for these applications and guide expectations. The results are plotted in Figure 6.8 for the different prediction methods. The best solution is not always found using all the cases, and sometimes better solutions are found with lesser numbers of cases. Surely the complete sample has all the information content of the smaller subsample. Yet, from a practical perspective,

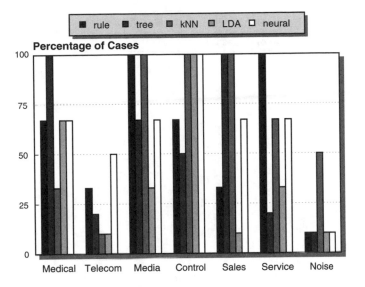

Figure 6.8: Percentage of Cases for Best Solution

learning with the full sample should usually find a solution near best, but a smaller subsample can sometimes do as well or even better.

The answer with the smallest test error may not fully hold up in the future, particularly for a changing population. This is an important consideration for methods like neural nets that consume large computational resources. Instead of finding the solution with the smallest error, an answer close to the best may also be considered equally valid. Is it possible to get a reasonable solution with a small subsample of cases? Reasonable is defined here as a solution within one standard error of the minimum-error answer found over all examined subsamples. Figure 6.9 graphs the percentage of cases for the smallest subsample size that gives a model within one standard error of the minimum-error solution. In only two situations does the selected answer use all the data.

We should be cautious about jumping to the conclusion that smaller percentages of cases are always adequate. These percentages are sampled from big data with thousands of cases, but even then, predictive performance can continue to improve for increasing numbers of cases.

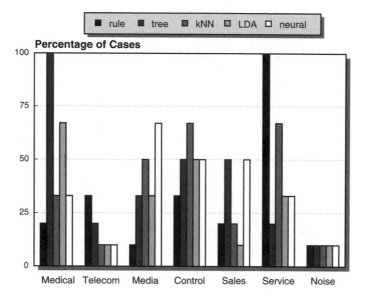

Figure 6.9: Percentage of Cases for "Near-Best" Solution

Some applications will have concepts that need more cases than can be found in any subsample. In the next section, we examine an incremental strategy that lets us determine the potential gains from additional cases. In practice, more data does not guarantee finding better answers. For secondary tasks, like tuning parameters for data reduction or for prediction methods, one can be fairly optimistic that smaller subsamples are adequate for tuning the methods.

6.5   Graphical Trend Analysis

While it has been demonstrated that competitive results are sometimes obtained with fewer cases, how do we know this without computing over all subsamples and the full set of cases? The optimum sample size is unknown prior to experimentation. One practical strategy is to examine proposed solutions as the size of the training set increases.

6.5.1　Incremental Case Analysis

A strategy that monitors the incremental change in errors can suggest the potential for additional gains in performance when the sample size is increased. An aggressive variation of an incremental strategy immediately stops when no incremental gain in error is found for an increased number of cases. A more conservative strategy may wait for a second confirmation, or may still continue learning on a pessimistic, low-priority basis. An incremental approach to learning starts with a large base of cases, and the increments differ substantially in the number of cases, not just percentages. Such factors as low prevalences, discrimination among many classes or difficult regression problems may suggest that larger increments of cases are needed.

An incremental strategy selects from more candidate solutions than can be found in fixed-sample learning. With one sample, most prediction programs will generate many solutions, and the one with the best performance on the test cases, Test1, is selected. An incremental strategy compares the selected solutions at increasingly larger sample sizes, measures their performance on the same test cases, selects the best one and tries to determine a trend.

The results of an incremental strategy are plotted in Figure 6.10. Learning halts when no gain is found for the most recent two increments. The incremental subsets are randomly selected from 10%, 20%, 33%, 50% and 100% of the training cases. Consecutive subsamples are random and are not required to be subsets of each other. The initial subset is the smallest of these percentages having at least 1,000 cases. The minimum increment of cases from one subsample to another is 1,000 cases. All decisions for the incremental strategy are made based on the test cases, Test1. The solution selected by the incremental strategy is evaluated on the totally hidden test set, Test2, and its performance compared to the baseline of training on all cases. When the number of cases is only moderately large, like for the control data, an incremental strategy is less enticing, and learning can commence on all cases.

For most of these applications, this incremental strategy terminates when using far fewer than the complete set of cases. The overhead is that several additional problems may need to be solved. The overall time taken by the incremental strategy is usually less than the time taken to solve a single problem for the complete set of training cases. This is

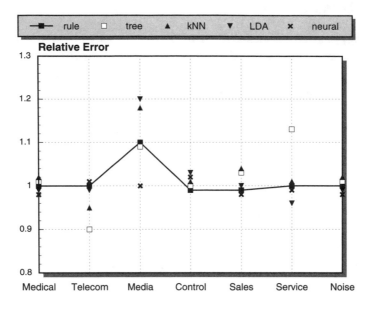

Figure 6.10: Performance of Incremental Case Analysis

illustrated in Figure 6.11, which plots the relative time taken by the incremental strategy compared to the baseline time for rule learning. For the control and service datasets, with only moderate numbers of cases, the all-case solution is needed to get the best answer; the subsample results have relative times greater than one. This is not surprising given the modest number of cases. In general for data mining, an incremental strategy speeds up learning. The speedup for computer-intensive methods such as neural networks is even more dramatic.

The empirical results suggest that an incremental strategy can be effective for mining big data. These results imply that there is a consistent trend for error as the number of cases increases. Error should generally decrease for large increments of cases. However, when the concepts inherent in the data are fully extracted, error should stop decreasing, with some variance from the minimum error. The trends for the tree's predictive performance with increasing sample size are illustrated in Figure 6.12. Results for other prediction methods are similar. For

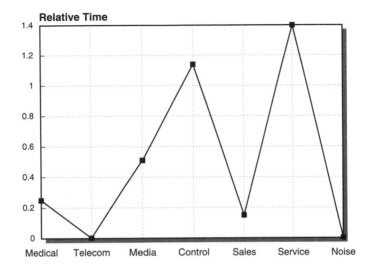

Figure 6.11: Speedups to Rule Learning by Incremental Analysis

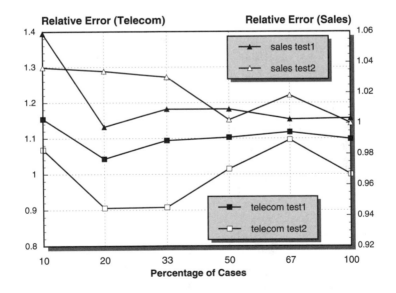

Figure 6.12: Trend for Incremental Tree Performance

some samples, particularly those with only moderate numbers of cases, the error continues to decline as the size of the subsample approaches the full sample. For other samples, typically very big data, the error first falls and then tends to reach a plateau, with some fluctuations as the subsample reaches the full sample. Solutions are selected based on independent test cases, Test1. The results on unseen cases, Test2, may not fully meet these expectations, because of sample variance for modest test sets or changes in population. The number of cases needed to stop learning depends on the complexity of the concepts implicit in the data. With big data, an incremental strategy should be quite helpful in gauging whether concept complexity has been exhausted, or more data are needed to grasp the concepts. In these applications, when the sample is very large, most concepts are quickly exhausted. For many prediction methods, especially the logic methods, solutions for increasing subsamples can be directly compared. They tend to converge to similar, sometimes identical solutions.

6.5.2   Incremental Complexity Analysis

The principal measure of predictive performance is error, and so far, all decisions have been based on an estimate of error. Another important quantity is the complexity of a solution. Data mining looks at big data. Despite their great dimensions, these data may have a small number of concepts, and performance is bounded by the predictive capability of these implicit concepts. Incremental complexity changes are quite useful in monitoring progress in mining, as are the relative changes in both error and complexity.

As the number of cases increases, error tends to decrease until little performance gain is made. For complexity, the opposite pattern emerges. With more data, more complex solutions may be found. As the number of cases increases, the complexity of solutions tends to increase. As the error curve plateaus, indicating that the induction of new concepts has been exhausted, complexity may stabilize, with a lingering tendency to increase. These trends may vary more for complexity than error. For a stable prediction method, differences in error usually will not vary greatly once error stabilizes. However, complexity is measured in much larger units, and results close in error can be far in units of complexity.

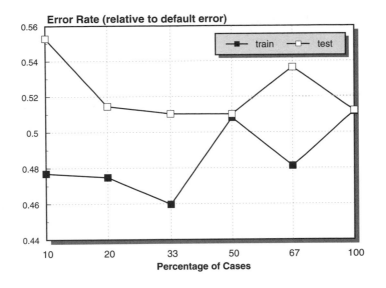

Figure 6.13: Error on Sales Data for Rule Solutions of Size 6

Figure 6.13 illustrates the trend for error when solution complexity, measured by rule components, is fixed at a modest level. Error is computed relative to the error of always picking the largest class. Eventually, sufficient data are available to exhaust the concepts producing this error. With increasing numbers of cases, the train and test errors eventually converge. It's not unusual for the training error to increase for a fixed degree of complexity. With more cases come more exceptions, and these exceptions are harder to fit in the same space. True error, as measured by test cases, remains fairly stable. The main hope of decreased error is to find a more complex solution. In Figure 6.14, a similar but more variable trend in error is observed. Here the trees are only approximately fixed in size (terminal nodes) over the different subsamples, and complexity is greater. Neural nets can be specified and trained for a fixed complexity, such as k hidden units. Although the training procedures for nets are sometimes unstable, the same incremental trend is observed.

The logic methods readily demonstrate the tendency for solution complexity to increase with more cases. Many data-mining problems will not

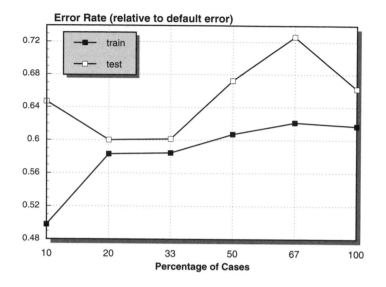

Figure 6.14: Error on Telecom Data for Tree Solutions of Size 21

have easy solutions. The logic methods approach problems expecting a complete solution that covers all cases, later scaling back to less complex solutions when they prove superior. In Figure 6.15, the number of terminal nodes are plotted for both the full covering trees and the minimum test-error trees. Covering trees can grow rapidly with a substantial number of cases. The size of the best-performing trees for increasing subsets of cases is relatively stable, but with a slight increase in complexity. The concepts implicit in the sample are found relatively early: the minimum-error tree is found at 20%, with the larger trees varying in performance at higher errors. A prediction method can potentially search the larger space of solutions supported by a larger sample. As a practical matter, not every solution can be examined, and for larger numbers of cases, many more complex solutions must be considered.

The dynamics of both error and complexity are illustrated in Figure 6.16, where the error and complexity of the selected neural net are contrasted with the error for a 2-hu (hidden unit) net on the telecom data. Error is measured relative to the baseline error on all cases. The

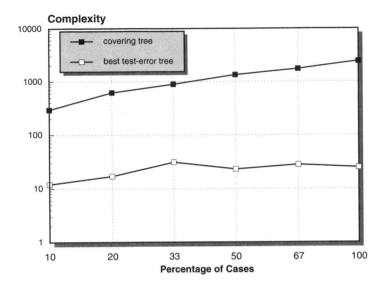

Figure 6.15: Incremental Solution Complexity for Trees

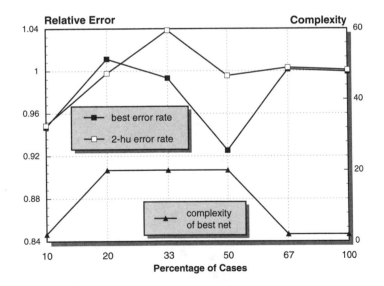

Figure 6.16: Incremental Neural Net Performance on Telecom Data

concepts inherent in the data are captured with only 10% of the cases. For larger subsets, the 2-hu net is not improving its test error. It's clear that its capacity for mining more cases is exhausted. The only hope for better performance is to increase complexity. The 20-hu net is selected for several subsets as best, but the evaluation shows little gain over the much lower complexity solutions. An incremental training strategy would have halted much sooner than the full set of cases.

The goal of complexity analysis is to find the right-size solution. When two solutions are close in performance, the lesser-complexity solution has some advantages: (a) more explanatory and (b) less variable performance on new data. With population changes, the reduced-complexity solution is probably the safer bet. When an incremental case strategy is used, the solution complexity can give valuable clues for the potential of better performance with more cases. These clues are also valuable for training when complexity is manually varied, such as in some forms of neural net or nearest-neighbor methods. For substantially increasing numbers of cases, expect to see some of the following trends:

- Training error stops decreasing for a specified complexity. Beyond this critical mass of cases, test error can still decrease until train and test error converge.

- Test error stops decreasing for a fixed-complexity solution, indicating a potential need for a greater-complexity solution.

- Test error decreases significantly, indicating a need for more cases.

- Test error decreases slightly with a major increase in solution complexity. More cases can be added to the training pool, but prospects for strong gains are limited.

- Test error stops decreasing for all solution complexities. Prospects are poor for significant gains in performance.

These are not inviolate scientific principles. They are expected trends that are observed in many applications, and they are subject to the vagaries of unstable prediction methods. These guidelines combine measures of error and complexity to help answer a key question for big data: how many useful concepts can be extracted from the data?

Method	Value	Feature	Case
rule	round50	step	incremental
tree	inc-ent	—	incremental
kNN	—	tree	incremental
LDA	—	step	incremental
neural	—	BAB	incremental

Table 6.3: Maximum-Reduction Strategies

6.6 Maximum Data Reduction

The goal of data reduction is to reduce data dimensions while preserving data concepts. Reduction techniques have been examined for reducing the three principal dimensions of data: (a) features, (b) values and (c) cases. So far, these techniques have been studied independently, and performance of each method has been compared to performance on the baseline results for the full data. Maximum reduction is achieved when appropriate combinations of these techniques are applied to the data. For example, feature selection can be used to delete features, value reduction can reduce the values of the remaining features and an incremental case analysis can be tried on the reduced data.

Many of the reduction techniques and prediction methods can be combined, but only some of these are good matches. For example, value reduction is usually restricted to the logic methods, and principal components to the other methods. Knowledge of a specific prediction method or knowledge of the data characteristics can heavily influence the choice of the applied reduction techniques. Instead of tuning these characteristics by prediction method or dataset, a uniform set of combinations is employed. For each prediction method, a reasonable combined reduction strategy is specified, and these techniques are consistently used for all applications. Thus, these results may be less than the best achievable by carefully matching techniques to prediction methods and data characteristics.

Table 6.3 describes the data-reduction strategy used for each prediction method. Figure 6.17 describes the results of these combined strategies. All results are plotted relative to the baseline error for the original

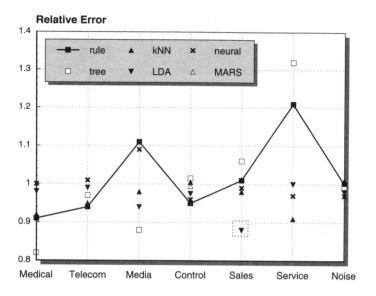

Figure 6.17: Maximum Reduction for Prediction Methods

data. For these data-mining applications, little is lost by moving head-long to maximum data reduction.

6.7   Are There Winners and Losers in Performance?

The same combined strategies for maximum reduction paint an approx-imate picture of competitive performance on these applications. In pre-vious sections, the relative error is computed from the baseline error of the same prediction method on the original data. In Figure 6.18, the baseline error is taken from the best result for any prediction method on the original data. These suggest that given big data, many prediction methods potentially produce competitive results. Occasionally, the lin-ear method is soundly outperformed by the nonlinear methods. Nearest-neighbor methods often do well with default distance measures, but sometimes are better served by specialized distance functions.

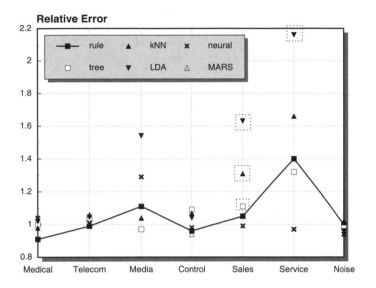

Figure 6.18: Competitive Performance of Prediction Methods

The results of Figure 6.18 are not conclusive for choosing data-reduction strategies and comparing prediction methods. The modern age of data mining is an age of tuning. With big data, sufficient test data should be available to select and evaluate alternatives. In this comparative study, no attempt is made to tune the reduction techniques or prediction methods. Usually this can be done on a modest number of training cases. For example, is rounding best at a maximum of 50 or 200 values? Should an unpruned tree be used for feature selection or should modest pruning be performed? Even without experimentation, the data characteristics may suggest a specific direction. For example, when the numbers of features or cases are modest, feature or case selection may be avoided.

The reduction techniques and prediction methods have been selected based on our own experiences or favorable reports in the research literature. The reduction techniques have their theoretical weaknesses, and should be considered tools that can be very effective when adequately applied and tested on real data. For the examined applications, few of the results for data reduction tested significantly different than those for the full data. When the empirical results are combined with knowledge of the prediction methods, some general conclusions may be reached.

For most logic methods, feature selection is nonessential, particularly when the number of features is not very large. For the other methods, like the neural networks and nearest-neighbor methods, feature selection is highly effective. Preprocessing the features often results in the prediction method finding a much more compact solution than that obtained from the original features. The stepwise method and principal components are the most robust for these prediction methods. Feature selection by a fully covering tree is a useful technique when it reduces the feature space. With many noisy features and lots of cases, tree-pruning methods are needed.

Value reduction is applicable to logic learning. The simple rounding method is a good performer, as are the other value-reduction methods. The incremental entropy strategy is often effective, but leaves less room for tuning, and entropy is unnatural for regression. Any of the schemes that do not use class information can be tuned to highly smooth the data or to reproduce the original data.

Incremental case analyses are effective for these applications. The main concerns are that the mining process halts too soon or that many unnecessary experiments are introduced. Such concerns can be alleviated by adopting a more cautious halting strategy or continuing experiments with weak expectations at lower priorities. Most of our applications did not yield complex solutions. Other applications—for example, classification problems with dozens of classes—may need much more data to exhaust their implied concepts.

6.8   Getting the Best Results

When applied to our applications, most prediction methods found competitive solutions. For these data, all signs point to an abundance of data relative to concepts that can be mined. Training and test errors are similar, the best solutions are of relatively low complexity and solutions do not improve much with increasing numbers of cases.

Some applications may have the opposite circumstances: not enough data relative to the concepts. Classification problems with many classes

Method	Letter	Digit	Smoothed-Digit
line	.2920	.1146	—
kNN	.0440	.0623	—
rule	.1122	.1286	.1246
neural	.0898	.0850	—
tree	.1214	.1550	.1634
bagging	.0704	.0977	.0992
arcing	.0360	.0693	.0713

Table 6.4: Voting Tree Solutions

tend to require larger numbers of cases, and such problems are not represented in our selection of data-mining applications. Averaging numerical answers for regression or voting answers for classification using solutions obtained from many random samples can produce very strong results, usually exceeding the performance of a single solution.

The most obvious candidate for averaging is the decision tree. Decision-tree methods induce solutions quickly, but these solutions can vary greatly from sample to sample. In our selected applications, solutions averaged over many samples usually have better results, but decreases in error were small because the limit has already been reached for extracting useful concepts. To illustrate the potential performance gains for averaged or voted solutions, two new applications are introduced: letter and digit. These are applications studied by others and shared with the research community. *Letter* is an alphabetic character-recognition application with 16 features, 26 classes, 15,000 training cases and 5,000 test cases. *Digit* is a decimal character-recognition application with 256 features, 10 classes, 7,291 training cases and 2,007 test cases. In Table 6.4, the results of a single solution on all training data are compared with voting answers from trees induced from randomly drawn bootstrap samples, *bagging*, or by adaptive resampling, *arcing*. Because of the extra time required to induce many solutions, also included are the results of rounding the digit data. Smoothing the values results in a tenfold speedup of learning. The letter features already have few values, so no further reduction is indicated. The results

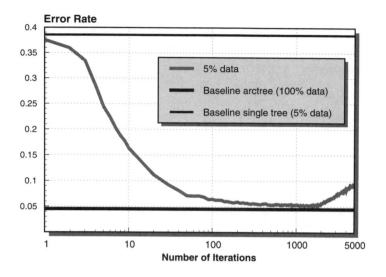

Figure 6.19: Arcing Trees from Subsamples of Letter Data

show a dramatic improvement over single solutions for trees by voting solutions of randomly drawn samples. Arcing has an edge over bagging, particularly when a small error is achievable. Also shown in Table 6.4 are the results of single solutions found by other methods. The results of voting the tree solutions rival the best single solutions found by other prediction methods.

The previous results were obtained from random samples drawn with the same number of cases as the training set. To illustrate the potential for case reduction when learning capacity is exceeded, 5% samples are drawn instead of the usual 100%. Thus, each solution is only found on 5% of the cases. As illustrated in Figure 6.19, with enough samples and solutions, the same performance can be attained by adaptive re-sampling as for much larger samples. This general result has important ramifications for data mining. Although a data warehouse may be huge, a random divide-and-conquer approach can be successful in matching or exceeding performance of solutions taken on larger samples or even a single solution obtained on the full warehouse. Besides the decision tree, most other prediction methods can greatly improve performance by voting and averaging many samples whose size is far less than the full capacity of the data warehouse.

6.9   Bibliographic and Historical Remarks

Published studies have compared prediction methods: [Weiss and Kulikowski, 1991; Ripley, 1993; Michie, Spiegelhalter and Taylor, 1994]. In contrast to those studies, the emphasis here is on data reduction and big data, not the prediction methods. The data-reduction techniques can readily be integrated into specific prediction models, but they also can be considered as general tools that are helpful across a broad spectrum of methods. The reduction techniques are statistical regularization techniques; complexity is varied to fit the data [Elder and Pregibon, 1996]. Data reduction shrinks the solution search space and smoothes the data. This often leads to improved results when the search space is reduced to the right size. With big data, the secondary objective is smoothing, and the primary goal is to reduce data without discarding the implicit concepts.

Visualization has played an important role in statistics and pattern recognition, where the data analyst has a decisive role [Scott, 1992]. Researchers in neural nets and the logic methods have been called tuners, often eschewing the visual approach for automated analysis. Visualization is most valuable for math methods where humans need a clearer understanding of the solution. Logic solutions, especially the less complex ones, are usually accessible without visual transformations. For big data, visualization techniques have weaknesses in deciphering high-dimensional data. The approach of this chapter could be called "visualization for tuners." The trends in performance of the solutions are presented, but the solutions are not directly visualized.

Visualization is critical to knowledge discovery, and database research has produced many effective techniques for displaying associational relationships. Highly innovative techniques to visualize hierarchical relations in decision trees or geographical relations are described in the data-mining section at SGI's web site.

Descriptions and samples of the letter data [Frey and Slate, 1991] and many other applications are available from the repository of machine learning databases at the web site of the University of California-Irvine. The digit zip code data are described in [LeCun et al., 1990].

7

Art or Science? Case Studies in Data Mining

The analysis of data should be based completely on scientific principles, but there are so many assumptions and unexpected variations that data mining may also be considered an art form. In the previous chapter, numerous hypotheses are tested in an antiseptic laboratory environment where most secondary influences are carefully controlled. Some of the datasets used in those experiments are simplified proxies for the real applications. Invoking the scientific method, researchers insist on a controlled environment to evaluate well-defined hypotheses. Even after the results are reported, other researchers may question their validity based on criticisms of the experimental procedures.

In the real world of data mining, we cannot expect this controlled laboratory setting. Many additional decisions must be made, from stating the problem and assembling the data, to tuning a prediction method for best performance. Dozens of experiments may be performed, and there is no assurance that the best solution will be found. These decisions may be based on empirical results or knowledge of the application. Whatever the role of artistic and heuristic decision making, the independent test data are always there to maintain objectivity. When final decisions are reached, they are supported by strong empirical evidence from data not directly used in the search for solutions.

Finding solutions is much more than running a prediction method over data. Chapter 6 is a scientific demonstration of alternative techniques that may lead to enhanced performance. To get a more realistic picture of real-world data mining, the applications should be examined in greater detail, starting with the goals of the projects and eventually arriving at useful solutions.

7.1   Why These Case Studies?

A study of data mining necessarily analyzes data from many applications. Artistic versus scientific perspectives on data mining lead to divergent selections of illustrative data for case studies. Statisticians have traditionally emphasized artificial data that are simulated from known distributions. Scientists like to control all factors in the experimental procedures. Researchers in data mining have emphasized real-world data. A collection of real data may be unbalanced or biased in some direction because the underlying statistical distribution is unknown. With enough test data, the evaluation of results can be very accurate. Arguing that the applications are representative of future applications is still problematic, whereas with artificial data, the space of samples can be controlled and varied.

For realistic data mining, the study of real-world data is essential. Profits, not pure science, are the driving forces. As illustrated in the comparisons of Chapter 6, real data are compatible with careful study. For data mining, these applications are more than fodder for a study. Each application has a story that should be understood as representative of real-world encounters with big data. Scientists may argue that these applications cover only a small part of the universe of applications. However, their explication is valuable for several reasons:

- The story may have similarities to your application story.

- The generic type of problem may be similar to yours.

- The steps taken to reach a solution may be the same as the steps needed to solve your application.

If real-world application is a defining characteristic of data mining, a split in scientific and commercial interests emerges. Scientists reserve the right to share data, expecting that they can replicate previous results and perhaps innovate and improve performance. A number of repositories of data used in research studies are accessible to the public. Repeated studies with these data have appeared in the literature. Unfortunately, these data are often not very large, and are generally of no commercial interest. The most obvious candidates for data mining are proprietary data that cannot be shared with outsiders.

Weighing these conflicting factors, we have assembled proprietary data that are not sharable. Proprietary data may best illustrate the art of data mining. Our goal is not to reach absolute conclusions, but to identify techniques that can be helpful for mining big data. We are familiar with these commercial applications, and can readily amplify on our experiences. The exact solutions are, however, proprietary.

Outside of a formal study, it is uncommon that many different prediction methods are applied to the same data. The application of the prediction methods is an important task in the overall process, but there are many other tasks. Many valid choices of prediction methods can be made, and many methods can readily be substituted for each other in our exposition. In these applications, the commercial customers had a keen interest in the logic methods and decision rules, which are the usual format for searching a database. While we use this representation in these case studies, the process of data mining with other prediction methods is similar.

7.2   A Summary of Tasks for Predictive Data Mining

An application has a story that motivates the data-mining efforts. Given a story and a source of data, the data-mining process has been organized into four tasks:

- Phase 1: Data Preparation

- Phase 2: Data Reduction

- Phase 3: Data Modeling and Prediction

- Phase 4: Case and Solution Analyses

Let's summarize the critical issues for these four phases of data mining.

7.2.1   A Checklist for Data Preparation

Data preparation, the subject of Chapter 3, is the transformation of raw or stored data into a standard form amenable to predictive data mining. We use a few characteristics of this process to summarize the data preparation for our applications:

- Raw form of stored data

- Goal

- Cases, features and transformations

- Time-dependencies

7.2.2   A Checklist for Data Reduction

Data reduction, the subject of Chapter 4, is the reduction of data to manageable proportions. We will use two characteristics of this second phase of data mining to summarize our applications and their solutions:

- Feature or value-reduction techniques

- Division of data for training and testing

Both data preparation and data reduction can be discussed without any assumptions of specific prediction methods.

7.2.3   A Checklist for Data Modeling and Prediction

A model for summarizing data and describing solutions is selected, and a prediction method is applied and tuned for best results. The characteristics of this phase of data mining are the following:

- Prediction method

- Adjustments of parameters

7.2.4 A Checklist for Case and Solution Analyses

Case and solution analyses are the final phase of data mining where the prediction methods are directly applied to the training data. The programs can train on the full set of cases or alternatively by incremental case analyses. Solutions are selected based on trade-offs of error and complexity. For our review of real-world applications, we describe the following characteristics of the case and solution analyses:

- Full or incremental case analysis

- Error and complexity review

- Solution assessment

7.3 The Case Studies

Four phases of data mining have been reviewed: data preparation, data reduction, data modeling and prediction and case or solution analyses. Each application has a story that justifies the expense of data mining. Figure 7.1 is the template for describing our data-mining case studies. The applications are reviewed from a generic data-mining perspective, with no assumptions of knowledge of the application area. In Chapter 6, data from these applications were used in a controlled laboratory exercise. Let's now look at these applications as real-world problems that have specific intellectual or commercial merit.

7.3.1 Transaction Processing

The Story

A long-distance telecommunications network processes massive numbers of transactions. Records of errors on the network are stored with the objective of mining these data to find trends and patterns that characterize faulty behavior. A worldwide network is an interconnected structure of complex devices with a huge number of different paths and circuits. Many sophisticated devices interact to achieve very high reliability, but errors occur and a record of these errors is made. Because of extensive redundancy and alternative paths, very few of these errors have an

The Story

Data Preparation:
>   *Raw form of stored data*
>   *Goal*
>   *Cases, features and transformations*
>   *Time-dependencies*

Data Reduction:
>   *Feature or value-reduction techniques*
>   *Division of data for training and testing*

Data Modeling and Prediction:
>   *Prediction method*
>   *Adjustments of parameters*

Case and Solution Analyses:
>   *Full or incremental case analysis*
>   *Error and complexity review*
>   *Solution assessment*

Figure 7.1: Template for Description of Case Studies

immediate effect on the transmission of data or voice communications. An acute problem is usually easy to determine. However, transient or chronic problems are difficult to pin down. For chronic faults, there is no immediate indication of a circuit problem. For transient faults, at the time a circuit is tested and measured, there may be no evidence of a continuing problem. The approach taken in this application is to look at a large sample of recorded problems to see whether there are patterns that are predictive of chronic and intermittent faulty behavior.

Data Preparation

Raw form of stored data.   Data are recorded in a coded alphanumeric format. Errors are logged with identifying information such as the type of error, the time and the connecting circuit.

Goal. Two classes are specified. The predicted class is chronic failure, which is defined as a circuit error in the week following an earlier period of errors. Chronic problems are low-prevalence events, but they constitute a much larger percentage of logged error messages. Errors are relatively rare. However, the number of telephone calls is huge, and errors can show up in large numbers over time.

Cases, features and transformations. A case corresponds to a circuit, that is, a path between two devices. A call from person A to person B may involve traversing many paths. The features are mostly counts of different types of errors on a circuit during a fixed time period, measured in days. For some features, the number of days having errors is much more predictive than the cumulative error count. Originally the stored data were scattered over disparate geographic locations and were collected by visiting databases at these locations. Eventually a data warehouse was constructed to store the universal set of information. The raw data are far from the standard spreadsheet form. Specialized preprocessing scripts and programs are written to scan the raw data over time and produce individual measured values for each circuit.

Time-dependencies. The data are constantly updated with new reports of logged errors. A single month's data are used for training, followed by continuing analyses of new data. A windowing scheme is used for measuring the time series for each circuit. Counts are made over a two-week period for the training data. The correct answer for a circuit is recorded from the data of the following week.

Data Reduction

Feature or value-reduction techniques. Value reduction is used. With only two dozen features and many cases, feature selection is not essential.

Division of data for training and testing. Initial experiments are performed with training data from one month and test data from the next month. Later experiments use the most recent month for test data, but also combine some training data from several previous months. The combined training months never improve results beyond the earlier results from a single month of training data.

Data Modeling and Prediction

Prediction method. Rule induction is selected as the primary method. However, experimental comparisons are made for several of the methods described in Chapter 5. Most prediction methods are competitive in performance.

Adjustments of parameters. Experiments on 10% of the data suggest that rounding with 50 values is effective. A number of program options are tried, but the baseline results with default values are the best.

Case and Solution Analyses

Full or incremental case analysis. Cases number in the tens of thousands. An incremental case analysis of the first two months of data gives a quick reading on the potential results and experiments. The prediction method is later run overnight on a full month's data. For follow-up months, a complete incremental analysis is not done beyond random subsampling up to about 33% of the cases. In addition, the best-performing solutions from the previous months' experiments are evaluated on newly arrived data.

Error and complexity review. An incremental case analysis shows that almost all of the error reduction can be obtained using no more than 10,000 cases. Complexity of the solution is relatively small, numbering about five patterns described as decision rules. For any given train and test period, it is possible to obtain a slight improvement in performance at the expense of greater complexity. The improvement generally disappears later when the next month's data are collected.

Solution assessment. Very predictive patterns of chronic problems are found. Results are consistent with specialized knowledge of the networks. The solution is remarkably stable over time, indicating that the types of problems causing the errors are not resolved, probably because they are considered low-priority problems. Many sets of decision rules are evaluated before a favorite is selected. Preference is given to solutions that have a lower percentage of false-positive errors.

7.3.2 Text Mining

The Story

The revolution in electronic publishing has invigorated empirical approaches to analyzing text. Using the metaphor of a vast library, electronic materials are indexed for future retrieval and possibly filtered to the personal interests of the individual reader. Unlike early attempts to understand concepts and sentence structure, text miners examine large samples of documents and accumulate frequency information in their search for discriminating phrases.

The application considered here is the classification of a large collection of newswire stories. A prepared list of hundreds of categories describes the classes. These categories can be used to retrieve relevant documents for specialized interests of the reader. Using only a sample of documents for training, the goal is to automatically classify and retrieve new documents without human intervention.

Data Preparation

Raw form of stored data. These data are electronic documents with topics assigned by humans. Multiple topics may be assigned to a story, for example, sports and football.

Goal. The goal is binary classification. There are hundreds of classification problems, one for each of the nonexclusive classes.

Cases, features and transformations. A case corresponds to a single document. The features are the most frequently used words in the sample for the given topic. Specialized programs and scripts are used to transform text into a standard spreadsheet form.

Time-dependencies. The time periods for samples must be carefully chosen. Frequency patterns can change over time. Topics that are of great interest in one period can appear less frequently in future periods. This also implies a moving strategy for updating cases, where new cases are added and older cases are discarded.

Data Reduction

Feature or value-reduction techniques.   Some approaches to text mining use only true-or-false features, indicating the presence or absence of a specific word in a document. Frequency information typically improves results slightly. When the obviously useless words are eliminated, the useful words rarely have high-frequency counts. Thus, an implicit form of value reduction is always present. Feature selection has been used successfully for document analysis, usually in conjunction with a single, universal dictionary for all topics. With potentially thousands of words in a dictionary, the tree-based feature selection is indicated. However, for this application, very large numbers of words are usually not essential, and an alternative is suggested: the k most frequent words for a given topic.

Division of data for training and testing.   It is essential to split the training and test cases by date of publication. The most recent cases are used for testing.

Data Modeling and Prediction

Prediction method.   Good results are achieved using methods from each of the three categories of prediction methods. The logic methods are particularly interesting for this application because the solution can readily be modified and verified by prior knowledge of important phrases.

Adjustments of parameters.   There are several parameters that can be tuned to improve results. These parameters are not tuned for each topic. Rather, the global best value over a large set of topics is used. For example, what is the value of k, the maximum number of words in a local dictionary? There are reasonable default values, such as $k = 150$, but tuning can improve results for some specialized topics.

Case and Solution Analyses

Full or incremental case analysis. Many topics are low-prevalence classes, and a full case analysis is indicated. For logic methods, learning is quick. For topics with large samples, an incremental analysis works well, sometimes providing simpler solutions.

Error and complexity review. As the sample size increases, it is not unusual to see a marginal improvement in error with a large increase in complexity. The population is not always stable over time, suggesting that the complex solutions are somewhat risky. In one collection of newswire stories, doubling the cost of false-negative errors improves results.

Solution assessment. Automated classification systems do very well for many topics, particularly when the categories have large samples and do not overlap. The topics that have been assigned by humans can readily be reviewed. We are all experts in reading most newswires, and there is ample room for disagreement with the assigned correct answer. This sampling approach to document classification has also been tried for German-language newswires with similar results.

7.3.3 Outcomes Analysis

The Story

Outcomes analysis is increasingly important in the highly competitive marketplace for health services, particularly given the pressures for cost containment. There are many alternatives for treatment, and of special interest is the efficacy of treatments relative to costs. For example, a comparatively inexpensive drug may reduce the need for expensive surgery. Instead of proving that a drug works to immediately ameliorate some physical problem, outcomes analysis evaluates the effectiveness and costs of competing treatments on large samples of patients over long periods of time. In laboratory medicine, an analogous rationale is presented for screening tests. Outcomes analysis should demonstrate that a reasonable number of patients who are subjected to the more expensive follow-up testing suggested by screening tests, in fact, have the tested ailment. An insurance company, government or medical plan would prefer not to pay for unnecessary tests. These data are assembled as part of a proprietary commercial effort to determine the predictive relationship between inexpensive screening tests and more expensive follow-up tests for an assumed healthy population.

Data Preparation

Raw form of stored data.   Most clinical laboratory data are readily accessible in standard form. Several problems arise for the retrieval of data from the commercial database. Some tests have several variations and are stored in different fields. Laboratory test screens are reported as positive real numbers, and negative numbers flag unusual results.

Goal.   The goal is classification. A class is a predicted high or low value for the more expensive, nonscreening test. The objective is to find a pattern in the screening tests by using a few tests that are known to be physically related to the potential medical problem. The experiments of Chapter 6 predicted a single test result, but the application has about a dozen candidate tests whose results might be predicted by the less expensive screening tests.

Cases, features and transformations.   A case is a series of measurements for an expected healthy patient. The data are borderline big, but from an application perspective, the sample is big because expensive testing on expected healthy patients is not reimbursable. It's easy to get such data for sick populations, but that does not fulfill the screening objective. Despite efforts to do a comprehensive job, many tests have missing values. In the experiments of Chapter 6, missing values are simulated in a manner consistent with medical knowledge of the tests. It is well known that the screening tests are not sufficiently predictive to produce an error rate better than always choosing the larger, healthy-population class. The prevalence of an abnormality is low, and false negatives are considered more serious than false positives. To overcome this dilemma, a number of techniques can be used, including (a) duplicating the small class cases to increase prevalence or cost of error; (b) lowering the goal threshold for indicating a high or low value; or (c) using specialized programs that search for solutions having low false-positive error rates.

Time-dependencies.   None.

Data Reduction

Feature or value-reduction techniques.   Value reduction using rounding improves results. The number of screening tests is small enough to reduce the need for feature selection.

Division of data for training and testing.   A reasonable division is 2/3 training, 1/3 testing.

Data Modeling and Prediction

Prediction method.   Logic methods are the likely candidates for this application. The acceptance of clinical testing results is based on high and low thresholds, which is consistent with logic methods. Weighted methods have not achieved great acceptance in many clinical applications.

Adjustments of parameters.   Mostly default options are used. Smoothing of training data is helpful.

Case and Solution Analyses

Full or incremental case analysis.   Sample size suggests an immediate full analysis.

Error and complexity review.   Current clinical practice prefers solutions with few screening tests, and these tests should be restricted to those that are known to be related by physical mechanism to the more expensive tests. Solutions can only be found when adjustments are made for the false-positive error rate instead of the global error rate.

Solution assessment. Patterns of inexpensive tests can screen for more expensive tests. These patterns find abnormalities that otherwise go undetected. The relatively high number of false positives reduces their effectiveness. Subjective judgments are made about the trade-offs of false positives to negatives, and about trade-offs of early detection of disease to the more expensive costs of advanced disease.

7.3.4   Process Control

The Story

Data from a large manufacturing plant process are collected and analyzed. A holding tank is used to store raw material for a large-scale manufacturing process. A human controller monitors the level of the product and makes adjustments to the controls that increase or decrease the level of raw material. If the holding tank overflows, a dangerous situation exists. If the holding tank reaches a critically low level, the manufacturing process must be halted and restarted—a difficult and expensive operation. The objective is to keep the material in the holding tank at an effective level based on various conditions including the rate of consumption of materials. There are a number of controls that the human controller can adjust, but only one of these has a dominant effect on the holding tank.

Data Preparation

Raw form of stored data. Instrument readings of plant conditions are recorded every 30 seconds. These data are a multivariate time series.

Goal. The problem is regression. The goal is to set the main control variable. This control variable is expressed as a single numerical variable that varies in both a positive and negative range. The sample values for the goal are actual changes in the control made by the human operator. These changes are not the optimal moves, which cannot be determined. As expected, most moves at 30-second intervals are "no change." A univariate solution using only the control variable would almost certainly fail. The solution is highly dependent on other values, such as the current level of the holding tank. Instead of using the current move of the controller, the net change from the control setting three minutes into the future is specified as the correct goal. This increases objectivity relative to the human move, which is often a small random move that is later countervailed.

Cases, features and transformations. The raw data are in standard spreadsheet form where the features are measured values for the instrument readings. Predictive performance can be improved greatly by transforming the raw data into moving averages and trends. Some of the raw measurements are also helpful. Instead of using all the cases, only those cases with major moves, greater than some absolute value, are included in the training and test samples. The smaller human moves are sometimes misleading and often inaccurate.

Time-dependencies. The application is an obvious time-series problem. Detection of trends in inflow and outflow of material are critical. If these are detected too late, disaster may strike with overflow of the tank or shutdown of the manufacturing operation.

Data Reduction

Feature or value-reduction techniques. The measured values are both integer and real-valued. The number of distinct values is quite manageable. However, some smoothing improves results.

Division of data for training and testing. If a plant changes operational procedures, results are affected. The number of cases is potentially very large, and the data are sampled from several different plants. The data are not sampled at the same time for each plant. The data could be divided into train and test cases by time, but this does not appear to be a necessity. A simple random division is adequate.

Data Modeling and Prediction

Prediction method. Rule induction gives an opportunity to match induced results with the general operational principles employed by the human operators. In terms of performance, weighted regression techniques have an advantage in minimizing error. However, the correct answer for the magnitude of the best move at any given time is not known. This leaves some room for subjective preferences in choosing a method.

Adjustments of parameters.   Of particular interest are the many variations of features and transformations of raw data that can be examined. The two major variations are (a) the number of time units for the moving averages and (b) the magnitude of moves used to define major moves. Only major moves are included in a sample.

Case and Solution Analyses

Full or incremental case analysis.   An incremental analysis is combined with method tuning to choose among the alternatives. For example, using a small magnitude for the definition of a major move greatly increases the number of cases. Examining a sample with small moves favors solutions that never make changes from current control variable settings. This is readily determined using a modest random subsample. The best variation of major-move cases drastically reduces the number of cases, and a full case analysis is then appropriate.

Error and complexity review.   Solutions at relatively low levels of complexity are found. The higher-complexity solutions are slightly better. For compatibility with plant operating procedures, the simpler solutions are preferred.

Solution assessment.   Given that the recorded values of the control variable are human moves made by different controllers, the excellent answers are somewhat surprising. Fewer than a dozen rules are needed to match relatively accurately the recorded control settings. A sample of major moves might be considered somewhat biased because the controls are not changed until a major move. Using the original data of measurements recorded every 30 seconds, the real-world operations are simulated for each proposed solution. Simulated performance is slightly less than suggested by the prediction programs but overall it remained excellent, avoiding all potential disasters.

7.3.5 Marketing and User Profiling

The Story

A key aspect of marketing is profiling potential customers so that marketing efforts can be directed to the best candidates for sales. In this application, the products are prescription drugs, and the sales targets are physicians. Pharmaceutical companies have representatives who meet with physicians to describe the merits of their products and leave product samples. The general objective is to direct the drug company representatives to physicians who will consider the merits of the company's drugs. After using some samples, these physicians will likely be interested in the company's products, and may increase the number of prescriptions written for their drugs.

Data Preparation

Raw form of stored data.   Data are found in several databases. A commercial service collects and supplies statistics on the sales per physician of prescription drugs. Additional sources supply background information, such as the specialty of the physician. The drug company maintains records of its sales force's visits and the number of samples that are left with a physician. These data are collected and pooled. The sales figures are numerical. The background information, such as the physician's specialty, is stored as alphanumeric codes.

Goal.   The application can be stated as a regression problem; the goal is to project physician sales for a specified drug during the next quarter. This formulation leads to poor results. Instead, the concept of physician market share is introduced, where the number of prescriptions for a drug is compared to the total number of prescriptions for its direct competitors. This market-share formulation leads to far improved results. While market share could be the goal for a regression problem, the best results are achieved when the application is stated as a classification problem with three classes for projecting market share for the next quarter: market share is up, down or approximately unchanged.

Cases, features and transformations.   Each case is a historical record for a physician. The data include weekly counts of drug sales for the last two years. Similarly, the number of visits and samples are also a time series for each case. Sales counts are transformed into market shares. The time series are summarized by many features, including counts from the most recent quarter, moving averages for several time periods and net changes in the two most recent quarters or other time periods. The background data, such as the physician's specialty, are transformed into true-or-false features.

Time-dependencies.   Many features are summaries of time series. The background features are static.

Data Reduction

Feature or value-reduction techniques.   The features can be broken into two groups: the counts and the background information. Extensive tuning can identify the best representations for the transformed market-share features. Given the reasonable dimensions, there is ample room for extra features composed from the counts and their transformations. Feature selection is helpful in eliminating many of the background features. For example, zip code information is available for each physician, and only a small subset of these are useful. Rule induction is used with dynamic feature selection and rounding.

Division of data for training and testing.   Data from the most recent quarter are used for testing, the remainder for training.

Data Modeling and Prediction

Prediction method.   This type of regression and time-series problem typically gets the linear treatment. The pharmaceutical company is interested in a logic approach that is potentially easiest to interpret and integrate into their current marketing strategies. Rule induction is used.

Adjustments of parameters. Tuning a prediction program's parameters usually leads to modest gains. Here, substantial gains are achieved by adjusting the time periods of the features. Consistent with the application literature on time series, the most predictive time periods are the most recent ones, and the earlier quarters add little to performance.

Case and Solution Analyses

Full or incremental case analysis. Sales figures are available for local geographic regions. Looking at one region at a time can be considered a natural type of incremental analysis. To get a quick overview of potential performance, a moderate percentage of cases is examined for each of three contiguous regions. A full case analysis of each region is then performed. Results are similar, but not identical. The data for the three regions are then pooled to provide a more general source of data.

Error and complexity review. Solutions are found at a modest level of complexity, about six decision rules per region. After reaching a plateau, increasing numbers of cases do not improve results. A low-complexity solution is desirable for use in a modified marketing strategy.

Solution assessment. Interesting patterns that are projected to future market share are found. For this application, the product sales trend indicates increasing market share, and the results of data mining are a pleasant experience. When a product is performing poorly, data mining may not provide positive feedback. Predicting likely future market share is one component in an overall strategy for marketing. Other factors, such as current market share, or the relationships between visits, samples and the market share, can influence an overall marketing strategy.

7.3.6 Exploratory Analysis

The Story

Application specifications are sometimes highly exploratory, and the stated goals are imprecise. Data on washing machine repairs for one of the largest vendors of these products are collected for a two-month period. Repairs to large consumer products are made in the consumer's home, often under warranty or service contract. One general objective is to anticipate the nature of repair problems, and to stock the right parts in the service vehicles so that repairs can be made in one visit.

Data Preparation

Raw form of stored data.   A data warehouse is not in place, and data are collected from multiple databases. In addition to the records of repairs, background information, such as model numbers and year of manufacture, are recorded in separate databases. The number of individual parts for the washing machines and dryers is large, numbering in the thousands. The parts' identifiers are recorded as alphanumeric codes. Up to 10 replaced parts can be recorded for a single service call, and these parts are recorded in no particular order. Information about the consumer's complaint is logged in a one-line text field. These data are compactly recorded in the databases as alphanumeric codes and text. The mapping of these fields into features for a standard spreadsheet form can produce a very large feature set. Given the exploratory nature of the application, the alphanumeric codes and text fields are treated as text, and the very same transformations for text mining are employed.

Goal.   The objectives of this project are exploratory, suggesting a series of classification goals. Each replacement part is specified as a classification goal, and the overall objective is to find a pattern in the replacement of specific parts. This type of experiment is repeated for each replaced part.

Cases, features and transformations.   A service call to fix a washing machine or dryer is a case. Some numerical features, such as the year of manufacture, are extracted directly from the databases. Most other features are binary transformations of the raw data using text-mining techniques.

Time-dependencies.   The given data are presented without explicit time relationships. For this problem, the best form of data presentation would be a repair history for individual machines. If the complete history is unavailable, the most recent set of related visits is still valuable for finding patterns in repeat visits. Here, historical information for individual machines is not obtainable, and the visits are treated as independent cases.

Data Reduction

Feature or value-reduction techniques. The feature space is drastically reduced by using the 200 most frequently found words or alphanumeric symbols in the database. The most frequently replaced parts or the most frequent user complaints are sufficient for a preliminary analysis.

Division of data for training and testing. The data are randomly split.

Data Modeling and Prediction

Prediction method. The client is most interested in specific logic patterns that they could readily understand, for example, that part X and Y are often replaced together.

Adjustments of parameters. Over 100 distinct classification goals and problems are specified. Given this number of experiments, the rule-induction program is used with its default settings.

Case and Solution Analyses

Full or incremental case analysis. Almost all of the experiments are mining of low-prevalence classes. With only moderate numbers of cases for the classes of interest, most of the problems can be solved relatively quickly even when using the full case set. Given the exploratory nature of the application, the problems are batched and run until completion.

Error and complexity review. These characteristics vary for the many experiments. The low-prevalence problems do not support high-complexity solutions. Solutions are found for many of the specified problems. Instead of weighing the merits of alternative solutions for any single problem, the larger task is to find some useful results in even a subset of the experiments. The results that appear most useful are those relationships that can be expressed as a simple conjunctions of events.

Solution assessment. Solutions are found to many of the over 100 classification problems. Most of these solutions are of little use. It is interesting to see that a prediction program can discover the governmental province of a local service center, or that a part fits a certain model washing machine. However, these relationships are clearly known to the vendor. Several useful associations are found, mostly of the form that parts A and B are usually replaced together. In addition, several phrases in the recorded consumers' complaints strongly suggest the types of repairs that are eventually made.

7.4   Looking Ahead

We have described data mining as a combination of art and science. Much of the science is well known, embodied in the prediction methods and the formal evaluation of results. Other key decisions are made in defining problems and preparing data, and these efforts cannot be described in exact terms. Surely our description of several real-world applications demonstrates the varied challenges faced by miners of data.

If we cannot assure the reader that data mining is an absolute science, then the usual cautionary questions may be asked. Is data mining a rehash of the same old analytical techniques? We feel confident that data mining is here to stay and the techniques can only improve. The age of big data is here. The Internet, intranets and proprietary data warehouses are omnipresent. Practical experience with mining such large volumes of data has been limited. This will soon change, and searching for and finding valuable patterns in data will be an essential ingredient in the workplace of the future.

7.5 Bibliographic and Historical Remarks

An iterative approach to applied classification is described in [Brodley and Smyth, 1997]. Data-mining techniques for telecommunications networks are discussed in [Sasisekharan, Seshadri and Weiss, 1996]. The proliferation of electronic publications and media has raised the profile of automated analysis of text [Apté, Damerau and Weiss, 1994] or personalized screening of documents [Sheth and Maes, 1993]. The results of an exploratory analysis for data collected from several databases for major appliance service records are presented in [Seshadri, Weiss and Sasisekharan, 1995].

Appendix:
Data-Miner Software Kit

The software option is a collection of routines for efficient mining of big data. Both classical and the more computationally expensive state-of-the-art prediction methods are included. Using a standard spreadsheet data format, this kit implements all of the data-mining tasks described in this book.

Availability

- Unix and Windows 95/NT

- Web distribution (license required to download)

Software Highlights

Data Preparation	editing normalization text transformation segmentation
Feature Reduction and Selection	significance testing tree selection
Value Reduction and Smoothing	rounding k-means clustering entropy
Case Reduction and Sampling	random bootstrapping/bagging adaptive/boosting voting/averaging
Prediction Methods: Classification and Regression	math - linear math - neural nets distance - nearest neighbors logic - decision trees logic - decision rules logic - association rules

For further details, visit http://www.data-miner.com or http://www.mkp.com/books_catalog/1-55860-403-0.asp.

References

[Agrawal, Imielinski and Swami, 1993] R. Agrawal, T. Imielinski and A. Swami. Database mining: A performance perspective. *IEEE Transactions on Knowledge and Data Engineering*, 5(6):914–925, 1993.

[Agrawal, Mannila, Srikant, Toivonen and Verkamo, 1996] R. Agrawal, H. Mannila, R. Srikant, H. Toivonen and I. Verkamo. Fast discovery of association rules. In U. Fayyad, G. Piatetsky-Shapiro, P. Smyth and U. Uthurasamy, editors, *Advances in Knowledge Discovery and Data Mining*, pages 307–328. AAAI Press, Menlo Park, CA, 1996.

[Apté, Damerau and Weiss, 1994] C. Apté, F. Damerau and S. Weiss. Automated Learning of Decision Rules for Text Categorization. *ACM Transactions on Office Information Systems*, 12(3):233–251, 1994.

[Baum, 1996] D. Baum. Data warehouse: Building blocks for the next millennium. *Oracle Magazine*, x(2):34–43, 1996.

[Brachman and Anand, 1996] R. Brachman and T. Anand. The process of knowledge discovery in databases: A human-centered approach. In U. Fayyad, G. Piatetsky-Shapiro, P. Smyth and U. Uthurasamy, editors, *Advances in Knowledge Discovery and Data Mining*, pages 37–58. AAAI Press, Menlo Park, CA, 1996.

[Breiman, 1996a] L. Breiman. Bagging predictors. *Machine Learning*, 24:123–140, 1996.

[Breiman, 1996b] L. Breiman. Bias, variance, and arcing classifiers. Technical Report 460, University of California, Berkeley, 1996.

[Breiman, 1996c] L. Breiman. Pasting bites together for prediction in large data sets and on-line. Technical Report, University of California, Berkeley, 1996.

[Breiman, Friedman, Olshen and Stone, 1984] L. Breiman, J. Friedman, R. Olshen and C. Stone. *Classification and Regression Trees*. Wadsworth, Belmont, CA, 1984.

[Brodley and Smyth, 1997] C. Brodley and P. Smyth. Applying classification algorithms in practice. *Statistics and Computing*, 7(1):45–56, 1997.

[Catlett, 1991] J. Catlett. On changing continuous attributes into ordered discrete attributes. In *Proceedings of the Fifth European Working Session on Learning*, pages 164–178. Springer-Verlag, Berlin, 1991.

[Chatfield, 1988] C. Chatfield. The future of time series. *International Journal of Forecasting*, 4:411–419, 1988.

[Chatfield, 1993] C. Chatfield. Neural networks: Forecasting breakthrough or passing fad. *International Journal of Forecasting*, 9:1–3, 1993.

[Cheng and Titterington, 1994] B. Cheng and D. Titterington. Neural networks: A review from a statistical perspective. *Statistical Science*, 9:2–54, 1994.

[Cleveland and Devlin, 1982] W. Cleveland and S. Devlin. Calendar effects in monthly time series: Modeling and adjustment. *Journal of the American Statistical Association*, 77(379):520–528, 1982.

[Cortes, Jackel, Solla, Vapnik and Denker, 1994] C. Cortes, L. Jackel, S. Solla, V. Vapnik and S. Denker. Learning curves: Asymptotic value and rate of convergence. In D. Touretzky, editor, *Advances in Neural Information Processing Systems, Volume 6*. Morgan Kaufmann, San Francisco, 1994.

[Dasarathy, 1991] B. Dasarathy. *Nearest neighbor (NN) norms: nn pattern classification techniques*. IEEE Computer Society Press, Los Alamitos, 1991.

[Dougherty, Kohavi and Sahami, 1995] J. Dougherty, R. Kohavi and M. Sahami. Supervised and unsupervised discretization of continuous features. In *Proceedings of the 12th Int'l Conference on Machine Learning*, pages 194–202, 1995.

[Elder and Pregibon, 1996] J. Elder and D. Pregibon. A statistical perspective on knowledge discovery in databases. In U. Fayyad, G. Piatetsky-Shapiro, P. Smyth and U. Uthurasamy, editors, *Advances in Knowledge Discovery and Data Mining*, pages 83–116. AAAI Press, Menlo Park, CA, 1996.

[Fayyad and Irani, 1993] U. Fayyad and K. Irani. Multi-interval discretization of continuous-valued attributes for classification learning. In *Proceedings of the 13th Int'l Joint Conference on Artificial Intelligence*, pages 1022–1027, 1993.

[Fayyad, Piatetsky-Shapiro and Smyth, 1996] U. Fayyad, G. Piatetsky-Shapiro and P. Smyth. From data mining to knowledge discovery in databases. *AI Magazine*, 17(3):37–54, 1996.

[Fildes and Makridakis, 1995] R. Fildes and S. Makridakis. The impact of empirical accuracy studies on time series analysis and forecasting. *International Statistical Review*, 63(2):289–308, 1995.

[Freund, 1995] Y. Freund. Boosting a weak learning algorithm by majority. *Information and Computation*, 121(2):256–285, 1995.

[Freund and Schapire, 1996] Y. Freund and R. Schapire. Experiments with a new boosting algorithm. In *Proceedings of the International Machine Learning Conference*, pages 148–156. Morgan Kaufmann, San Francisco, 1996.

[Frey and Slate, 1991] P. Frey and D. Slate. Letter recognition using holland-style adaptive classifiers. *Machine Learning*, 6(2), 1991.

[Friedman, 1991] J. Friedman. Multivariate adaptive regression splines. *Annals of Statistics*, 19(1):1–141, 1991.

[Friedman, 1995] J. Friedman. An overview of predictive learning and function approximation. In V. Cherkassky, J. Friedman and H. Wechsler, editors, *From Statistics to Neural Networks: Theory and Pattern Recognition*. Springer-Verlag, Berlin, 1995.

[Friedman and Stuetzle, 1981] J. Friedman and W. Stuetzle. Projection pursuit regression. *J. Amer. Stat. Assoc.*, 76:817–823, 1981.

[Hansell, 1995] S. Hansell. Need a loan? Ask the computer. *New York Times*, April 18:D1, 1995.

[Hart, 1967] P. Hart. The condensed nearest neighbor rule. *Transactions on Information Theory*, IT-14:515–516, 1967.

[Hartigan and Wong, 1979] J. Hartigan and M. Wong. A k-means clustering algorithm, ALGORITHM AS 136. *Applied Statistics*, 28(1), 1979.

[Heckerman, 1996] D. Heckerman. Bayesian networks for knowledge discovery. In U. Fayyad, G. Piatetsky-Shapiro, P. Smyth and U. Uthurasamy, editors, *Advances in Knowledge Discovery and Data Mining*, pages 273–306. AAAI Press, Menlo Park, CA, 1996.

[James, 1985] M. James. *Classification Algorithms*. Wiley, New York, 1985.

[Kimball, 1996] R. Kimball. *The Data Warehouse Toolkit: Practical Techniques for Building Dimensional Data Warehouses*. Wiley, New York, 1996.

[Kolata, 1994] G. Kolata. New frontier in research: Mining patient records. *New York Times*, August 9:A20, 1994.

[Kolodner, 1993] J. Kolodner. *Case-Based Reasoning*. Morgan Kaufmann, San Francisco, 1993.

[LeCun et al., 1990] Y. LeCun, B. Boser, J. Denker, D. Henderson, R. Howard, W. Hubbard and L. Jackel. Handwritten digit recognition with a back-propagation network. In D. Touretzky, editor, *Advances in Neural Information Processing Systems, Volume 2.* Morgan Kaufmann, San Francisco, 1990.

[Lewis, 1992] D. Lewis. Text representation for text classification. In P. Jacobs, editor, *Text-Based Intelligent Systems*. Lawrence Erlbaum, Hillsdale, NJ, 1992.

[Makridakis et al., 1984] S. Makridakis, A. Andersen, R. Carbone, R. Fildes, M. Hibon, R. Lewandowski, J. Newton, E. Parzen and R. Winkler, editors. *The Forecasting Accuracy of Major Time Series Methods*. Wiley, New York, 1984.

[Makridakis et al., 1993] S. Makridakis, C. Chatfield, M. Hibon, M. Lawrence, T. Mills, K. Ord and K. Simmons. The M2 competition: A real-time judgementally based forecasting study. *International Journal of Forecasting*, 9:5–22, 1993.

[Masters, 1995] T. Masters. *Neural, Novel and Hybrid Algorithms for Time-Series Prediction*. Wiley, New York, 1995.

[Mehta, Agrawal and Rissanen, 1996] M. Mehta, R. Agrawal and J. Rissanen. SLIQ: A fast scalable classifier for data mining. In *Proceedings of the Fifth Int'l Conference on Extending Database Technology*, pages 18–32, 1996.

[Michie, Spiegelhalter and Taylor, 1994] D. Michie, D. Spiegelhalter and C. Taylor. *Machine Learning: Neural and Statistical Classification*. Ellis Horwood, New York, 1994.

[Miller, Todd and Hedge, 1989] G. Miller, G. Todd and S. Hedge. Designing neural networks using genetic algorithms. In *Proceedings of the Third Int'l Conference on Genetic Algorithms*. Morgan Kaufmann, San Francisco, 1989.

[Murtagh and Heck, 1987] F. Murtagh and A. Heck. *Multivariate Data Analysis*. Kluwer Academic, Dordrecht, 1987.

[Narenda and Fukunaga, 1977] P. Narenda and K. Fukunaga. A branch and bound algorithm for feature subset selection. *IEEE Transactions on Computers*, C-26:917–922, 1977.

[Piatetsky-Shapiro, Brachman, Khabaza, Kloesgen and Simoudis, 1996] G. Piatetsky-Shapiro, R. Brachman, T. Khabaza, W. Kloesgen and E. Simoudis. An overview of issues in developing industrial data mining and knowledge discovery applications. In *Proceedings of the Second International Conference on Knowledge Discovery and Data Mining*, pages 89–95, 1996.

[Quinlan, 1989] J. Quinlan. Unknown attribute values in induction. In *International Workshop on Machine Learning*, pages 164–168, Ithaca, NY, 1989.

[Quinlan, 1996] J. Quinlan. Bagging, boosting, and c4.5. In *Proceedings of American Association on Artificial Intelligence*, pages 725–730, 1996.

[Ridout, 1988] M. Ridout. An improved branch and bound algorithm for feature subset selection. *Applied Statistics*, 37(1):139–144, 1988.

[Ripley, 1993] B. Ripley. Statistical aspects of neural networks. In O. Barndorff-Nielsen, J. Jensen and W. Kendall, editors, *Networks and Chaos — Statistical and Probabilistic Aspects*, pages 40–123. Chapman and Hall, London, 1993.

[Ripley, 1994] B. Ripley. Neural networks and related methods for classification. *Journal of the Royal Statistical Society, Series B*, 56(3):409–456, 1994.

[Saraee and Theodoulidis, 1995] M. Saraee and B. Theodoulidis. Knowledge discovery in temporal databases. In *IEE Colloquium on Knowledge Discovery in Databases*, pages 1–4, 1995.

[Sasisekharan, Seshadri and Weiss, 1996] R. Sasisekharan, V. Seshadri and S. Weiss. Data mining and forecasting in large-scale communication networks. *IEEE Expert — Intelligent Systems*, 11:37–43, 1996.

[Scott, 1992] D. Scott. *Multivariate Density Estimation: Theory, Practice, and Visualization*. Wiley, New York, 1992.

[Seshadri, Weiss and Sasisekharan, 1995] V. Seshadri, S. Weiss and R. Sasisekharan. Feature extraction for massive data mining. In *Proceedings 1st International Conference on Knowledge Discovery and Data Mining*, pages 258–262, 1995.

[Sheth and Maes, 1993] B. Sheth and P. Maes. Evolving agents for personalized information filtering. In *Proceedings of the IEEE CAIA-93*, pages 345–352, 1993.

[Tansel et al., 1993] A. Tansel, J. Clifford, S. Gadia, S. Jajodia, A. Segev and R. Snodgrass, editors. *Temporal Databases: Theory, Design, and Implementation*. Benjamin Cummings Co., Redwood City, CA, 1993.

[Tukey, 1977] J. Tukey. *Exploratory Data Analysis*. Addison Wesley, Reading, MA, 1977.

[Weiss and Indurkhya, 1993] S. Weiss and N. Indurkhya. Optimized Rule Induction. *IEEE Expert*, 8(6):61–69, 1993.

[Weiss and Indurkhya, 1995] S. Weiss and N. Indurkhya. Rule-based machine learning methods for functional prediction. *Journal of Artificial Intelligence Research*, 3:383–403, 1995.

[Weiss and Kulikowski, 1991] S. Weiss and C. Kulikowski. *Computer Systems That Learn: Classification and Prediction Methods from Statistics, Neural Nets, Machine Learning, and Expert Systems*. Morgan Kaufmann, San Franscisco, 1991.

[Wolpert, 1992] D. Wolpert. Stacked generalization. *Neural Networks*, 5:241–259, 1992.

Author Index

Subject Index